Office 2013

for

Seniors

in
easy steps

Also covers Office 365 subscription editions

In easy steps is an imprint of In Easy Steps Limited
16 Hamilton Terrace · Holly Walk · Leamington Spa
Warwickshire · United Kingdom · CV32 4LY
www.ineasysteps.com

Notice of Liability
Every effort has been made to ensure that this book contains accurate
and current information. However, In Easy Steps Limited and the
author shall not be liable for any loss or damage suffered by readers
as a result of any information contained herein.

Trademarks
Microsoft® and Windows® are registered trademarks of Microsoft
Corporation. All other trademarks are acknowledged as belonging to
their respective companies.

In Easy Steps Limited supports The Forest Stewardship Council (FSC),
the leading international forest certification organisation. All our titles
that are printed on Greenpeace approved FSC certified paper carry the
FSC logo.

MIX
Paper from
responsible sources
FSC® C020837

Printed and bound in the United Kingdom

ISBN 978-1-84078-582-1

Contents

3 Complex Documents   47

4 Calculations   69

5 Manage Data 87

6 Presentations 109

7 Office Extras 129

8 Email 147

9   Time Management   167

10   Manage Files and Fonts   189

1 Introducing Office 2013

This chapter discusses the latest version of Microsoft Office, with its ribbon style of user interface. It identifies the range of editions, and outlines the requirements for installation, starting applications, shared features, Office document types and compatibility with older versions.

There's no upgrade pricing for retail Office 2013 editions, and they provide a license for use on one computer only, though you can transfer the license if you replace your machine.

All of the Office 2013 applications are also available in the Office 365 editions on a subscription basis, and these have licenses for up to five computers.

See page 222 for more details of the options for Office 2013.

Microsoft Office 2013

Microsoft Office is a productivity suite of applications that share common features and approaches. There have been numerous versions, including Office 95, Office 97, Office 2000, Office XP (aka Office 2002), Office 2003, Office 2007 and Office 2010. The latest version, released in January 2013, is Microsoft Office 2013.

There are various editions, with particular combinations of applications. The Home and Student edition contains:

- Excel 2013   Spreadsheet and data manager
- PowerPoint 2013   Presentations and slide shows
- OneNote 2013   For taking and collating notes
- Word 2013   Text editor and word processor

There's a Windows RT (for mobile devices) version of the Home and Student edition, though the applications it provides have restricted feature sets.

The Home and Business edition of Office 2013 contains all of the applications in the Home and Student edition, plus:

- Outlook 2013   Electronic mail and diary

The Professional edition of Office 2013 contains all those found in Home and Business edition, plus two applications:

- Access 2013   Database manager
- Publisher 2013   Professional document creation

For business users there are two volume license editions. The Standard edition has all the applications from the Professional edition except for Access. The Professional Plus edition has all the products from the Professional edition with two additions:

- InfoPath 2013   Design electronic forms
- Lync 2013   Online messaging service

Ribbon Technology

Whichever edition of Office 2013 or Office 365 that you have, the applications they provide will feature the Ribbon graphical user interface, which replaces menus and toolbars.

This shows the Ribbon in Word 2013, with the Home tab selected. This tab usually displays five groups associated with basic document creation – Clipboard, Font, Paragraph, Styles and Editing. Some additional contextual tabs appear when appropriate. Each group contains a set of related commands and icons.

The Ribbon contains command buttons and icons, organized in a set of tabs, each containing groups of commands associated with specific functions. This makes the features more intuitive, and more readily available, and allows you to concentrate on the tasks you want to perform rather than the details of how you will carry out the activities.

Some tabs are contextual and appear only when certain objects are selected. For example, when you select an image, the Picture Tools Format tab and its groups are displayed.

This shows the Picture Tools Format group which is added to the Home tab in Word 2013, when you select an inserted picture.

The Ribbon-based user interface also features extended ScreenTips with images and links. The tips display as you move the mouse pointer over an option, and describe what the functions are or give keyboard shortcuts.

This result-oriented user interface was first introduced in Office 2007, and now appears in all the applications in Office 2013.

For systems with touch-enabled monitors, Office 2013 offers a Touch mode ribbon with larger and more widely spaced icons (see page 16).

Beware

These are minimum requirements. It would be better to have a higher-speed processor, with additional memory and, for Windows 8 systems, a touch-enabled monitor.

Don't forget

These system properties are for the PCs used for this book, the Dell Inspiron 560 64-bit desktop (Windows 8 Pro and Office Professional Plus) and the Microsoft Surface RT 32-bit Tablet (Windows RT and Office 2013 RT). Systems with Windows 8.1 are similar. However, the tasks and topics covered will generally apply to any edition or operating environment.

What's Needed

To use Microsoft Office 2013, you will need at least the following components in your computer:

- 1GHz processor (32-bit or 64-bit)

- 1GB memory (32-bit)
  2GB memory (64-bit)

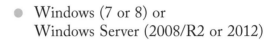

- 3.0GB available disk space

- 1024 × 576 or larger resolution monitor

- Windows (7 or 8) or
  Windows Server (2008/R2 or 2012)

Some functions will have additional requirements, e.g.:

- Touch-enabled monitor for controlling the system

- Internet connection for online help

- CD-ROM or DVD drive for install, data and backup

Windows 8 or RT systems will fully support Office 2013.

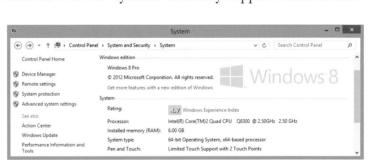

Installing Office 2013

If you purchase a copy of Office 2013, it will be downloaded onto your computer from where you can burn a DVD. Run the Setup program from this disc to begin the installation.

1 Accept license terms for Office 2013 as prompted

2 Select Install Now to accept the default settings and install all the Office 2013 applications in your edition

3 Applications are installed and Office 2013 finalized

4 Tiles for all your Office 2013 applications will be added to the Start screen

Select Customize to choose which particular applications you want to install, or to specify the 64-bit version of Office 2013. By default, the 32-bit version is installed, even if there is a 64-bit operating system.

If you have an older version of Office, you may be offered the option to Upgrade the existing installation.

Start an Application

The first time you start an application after installing Office 2013, you are prompted to complete the installation settings.

Hot tip

This shows the Windows 8 Start screen. However, equivalent shortcuts are added to the Windows 7 Start menu.

1 Switch to the Start screen and select an application, e.g. Word

2 You'll be prompted to Activate Office

3 Enter your email address for a subscription to Office 365 and click Next

4 For a purchased Office 2013, click Enter a product key, type your license key and click Continue

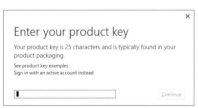

Don't forget

Setting up and activating the first application in Office sets up all the other applications in the suite at the same time.

5 Select Use recommended settings, click Accept then choose Office Open XML formats and click OK

...cont'd

You can also add shortcuts for the Office applications to the Taskbar on the Desktop. To create the shortcuts:

1 On the Start screen, right-click the application tile and select Pin to taskbar from the App bar displayed

If you have Windows RT and Office RT on your computer, you'll find that the shortcuts for Word, Excel, PowerPoint and OneNote are already defined for the Taskbar.

2 Repeat to add any other applications that you want readily available

3 Press Escape to return to the Start screen and click the Desktop tile to see the revised Taskbar

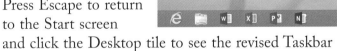

4 If any of your applications are not displayed on the Start screen, right-click the screen and select All apps

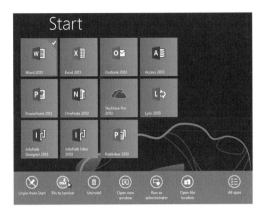

The applications that are listed on the Apps screen depend on the edition of Office 2013 you have installed, e.g. there are 19 entries for Office 2013 Professional Plus, but only 7 for Office RT.

5 Right-click any application and select Pin to taskbar to add a shortcut (or click Pin to Start)

Application Start

Document-based Office applications open at the Start screen with the Recent Documents list and various Templates.

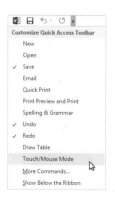

The Touch/Mouse Mode button appears by default when you have a touch-enabled monitor. To add it if not displayed, click the Customize Quick Access Toolbar button and then select Touch/ Mouse Mode. You can then display the enlarged Ribbon on a standard monitor.

1 Select an application tile such as Word or select the equivalent icon from the Taskbar to display the application Start screen

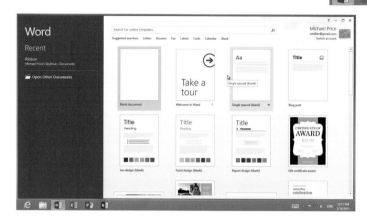

2 Select the blank document to begin an edit session

3 Click the Touch/Mouse Mode button on the Quick Access Toolbar and select Touch

4 The expanded Ribbon is displayed

The Application Window

When you start Excel, PowerPoint or Word, the program window is displayed with a blank document named Book1, Presentation1, or Document1, respectively. E.g. in Word:

BackStage (File tab) Quick Access toolbar Document name Tabs

Help button

Ribbon Display options

Minimize/Restore/Close

Ribbon icons (display lists or galleries)

Collapse the Ribbon

Launch button (shows dialog box)

Vertical scroll bar

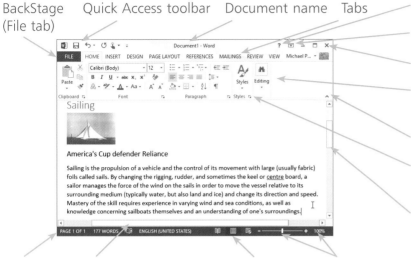

Status bar Horizontal scroll bar View buttons Zoom level

When you update your document, click File to display the BackStage and select Save to name and save the document in your SkyDrive (see page 18) or on your computer.

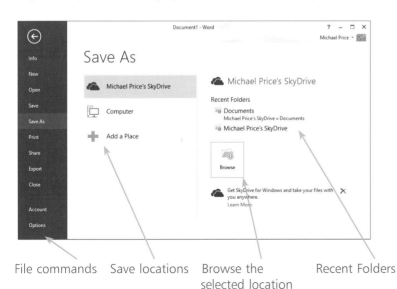

File commands Save locations Browse the selected location Recent Folders

Hot tip

The Save As dialog will open the first time you select Save for a new document.

Don't forget

From the BackStage you can select Info for details about your document, or New to start another document, or Open to display an existing document. There are also printing and sharing options provided.

Your SkyDrive

To save your documents to your SkyDrive online storage:

1 Select File, Save As, choose your SkyDrive and click the Browse button

When you set up a Microsoft Account to sign on to Windows 8, or Windows RT you are assigned an allowance of up to 7GB online storage (*at the time of printing*) which is managed on the Microsoft SkyDrive server (see page 225).

2 Confirm or amend the document name then choose the appropriate folder, e.g. Documents

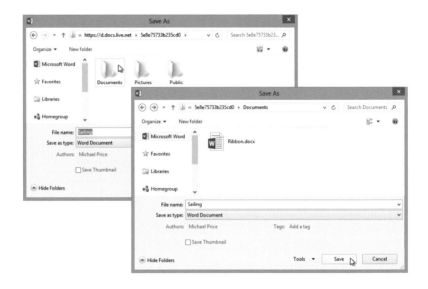

This means that you can access and edit the documents from any computer where you sign on with the same Microsoft account. You can also access your SkyDrive and documents from your browser.

3 Click Save to upload the document and save it to your SkyDrive folder

4 To access your SkyDrive from your browser, go to web page **www.skydrive.com**, and sign in if needed

...cont'd

If you are running Windows 8 (or Windows 7) you can download SkyDrive for Windows and keep a local copy so you can edit documents even when not Internet connected.

1 From File, Save As click the option to Learn More about SkyDrive for Windows

Don't forget

If you have Windows RT, this application is not available, and you cannot automatically sync a local copy of your SkyDrive.

2 Select Download now, and click Run as prompted

Hot tip

3 The application is downloaded and installed, and the local SkyDrive is created

You'll be offered the option to sync all your files and folders on the SkyDrive, or to choose folders to sync.

4 You find a link to the local SkyDrive under Favorites in File Explorer, and it is here that Office 2013 will now save documents when you select SkyDrive

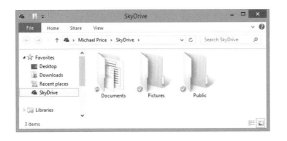

Live Preview

With the Ribbon interface, you can see the full effect on your document of format options such as fonts and styles, by simply pointing to the proposed change. For example, to see font formatting changes:

In previous versions, you would be shown a preview of the new font or style using a small amount of sample text. Office 2013 displays full previews.

1 Highlight the text that you may wish to change, then select the Home tab

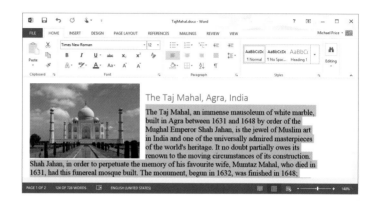

2 Click the arrow next to the Font box and move the mouse pointer over the fonts you'd like to preview

The selected text is temporarily altered to show the font (or the font size, color or highlight) that you point to.

3 Click the font to apply the change to the text, or press Escape to finish viewing options

4 Similarly, preview the effects of Text Highlight Color, Font Color, Styles, etc.

Working With the Ribbon

The Ribbon takes up a significant amount of the window space, especially on lower-resolution displays. To hide it:

1 Click Collapse the Ribbon (see page 17) or Right-click the tab bar and select Collapse the Ribbon

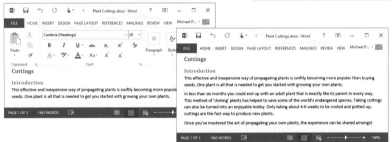

2 The Quick Access toolbar and the Tab bar will still be displayed while the Ribbon is minimized

3 The Ribbon reappears temporarily when you click one of the tabs, so you can select the required item

4 Alternatively, press and release the Alt key to display keyboard shortcuts for the tabs

5 Press Alt + shortcut key, for example Alt + H, to select Home and display the Ribbon and shortcuts

Hot tip

You can also select Ribbon Display Options on the Titlebar and choose Show Tabs to hide the Ribbon, or Show Tabs and Commands to reveal the Ribbon.

Don't forget

Hold down the Alt key and press the keys in sequence, for a two-letter shortcut, such as Alt + FS (Font Size) shown when you select the Home tab, and press Esc to go back up a level.

Quick Access Toolbar

The Quick Access toolbar contains commands independent of the selected tab. There are five buttons initially:

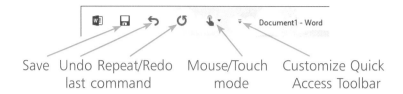

Save   Undo Repeat/Redo   Mouse/Touch   Customize Quick
            last command   mode   Access Toolbar

Hot tip

The Save As dialog will open the first time you press the Save button for a new document.

1 Click the Save button to write the current contents of the document to the SkyDrive or to the PC drive

2 Click Repeat to carry out the last action again, or click Undo to reverse the last action, and click again to reverse the previous actions in turn

Hot tip

You can right-click any command on the Ribbon and select Add to Quick Access Toolbar.

3 When you have pressed Undo, the Repeat button changes to become Redo which will re-apply actions you have reversed

4 Click the Customize button to add or remove icons, using the shortlist of frequently-referenced commands

5 Click More Commands... to display the full list of commands, then add and remove entries as desired

Don't forget

You can also click the File tab, then select the application Options and select Quick Access Toolbar to display this dialog box.

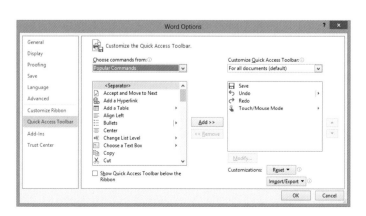

Office Document Types

The objects you create using the Office applications will be office documents of various types, including:

- Formatted text and graphics   Word document
- Flyers and brochures   Publisher publication
- Spreadsheets and data lists   Excel worksheet
- Presentations and slide shows   PowerPoint presentation

Each item will be a separate file. By default, they are saved in the Documents library for your username (logon ID).

1   To review files, click File Explorer on the Desktop and select Libraries, Documents

2   This shows files as large icons. For another style, click the View tab and select, for example, Details, to show file information, e.g. date modified, size, type

Note that, in some applications, groups of related items will be stored together in a specially structured file. For example:

- Data tables, queries and reports   Access database
- Messages, contacts and tasks   Outlook folders
- Notes and reminders   OneNote folders

The Documents library consists of the Documents folder for the current user, and the Public (shared) Documents folder.

23

You can specify another folder or subfolder for particular sets of documents, to organize the contents of your libraries.

File Extensions

You can also change Folder Options in the Control Panel, under Appearance and Personalization.

To see the file extensions that are associated with the various document types:

1 In File Explorer, select the View tab and in the Show/Hide section of the Ribbon click the box labeled File names extension

2 View the contents of your library folder

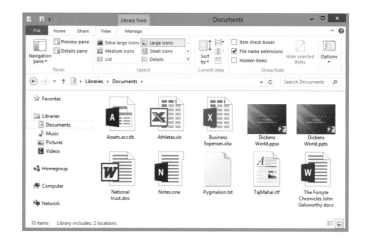

Don't forget

Files saved in Office 2013 use OpenXML formats and extensions, for example .docx and .xlsx. Older Office files will have file types such as .doc and .xls.

3 The file type will be shown, along with the file name, whichever folder view you choose

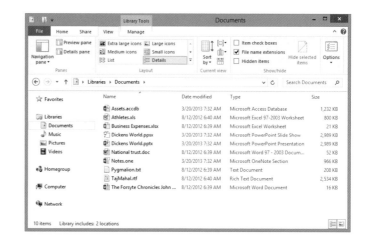

Compatibility Mode

Office 2013 opens documents created in previous versions of Office applications, for example .doc (Word) or .xls (Excel).

1 Click File and select Open, then click the down arrow for document type to list the types supported

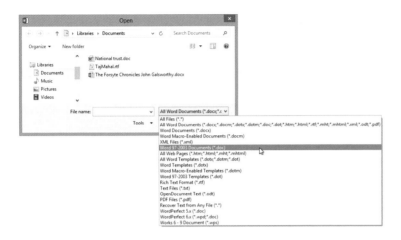

2 Choose the document type, Word 97–2003 for example, then select the name, e.g. National Trust.doc

Compatibility Mode

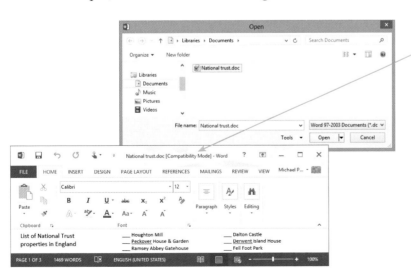

3 Documents from previous versions (including .docx files from Word 2010) open in Compatibility Mode

Convert to Office 2013

If you have opened a document in Compatibility Mode, you can convert it to the standard Office 2013 format.

1 Select File tab and Info and click the Convert button

You can also click the File tab, select Save As, and choose the standard Office format (e.g. Word Document) to carry out the conversion.

Converting will create a file of the same name, but with the new Office 2013 format extension. The original file will be deleted.

2 Click OK to confirm, and the file type is amended

3 To replace the original file, select File and then Save

With Save As, you have the option to change the file name, and the location for the new document.

4 To retain the original and create a new file in Office 2013 format, select File, then Save As, and click Save

2 Create Word Documents

This covers the basics of word processing, using the Word application in Office 2013 – enter, select and copy text, save and autosave, and proof text. It looks at the use of styles to structure the document, and adding document features, such as pictures, columns, and word counts, creating tables, the use of Paste Special, and the facilities for printing.

Create a Word Document

There are several ways to create a Word document:

1 Right-click an empty space in the Documents folder and select New, Microsoft Word Document

New Microsoft Word Document

2 Start Word and select the Blank document (see page 16) to create a document initially called Document1

3 If Word is open, select the File tab, click New and click the Blank document to create a new document

Enter Text

1 Click on the page and type the text that you want. If the text is longer than a single line, Word automatically starts the new line for you

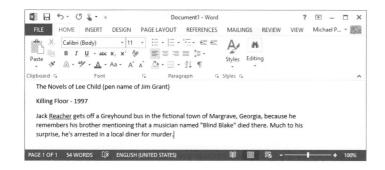

You can copy and paste text from other sources, such as web pages. Use Paste Options (see page 31) to avoid copying styles and formats along with the text.

2 Press Enter when you need to insert a blank line or start a new paragraph

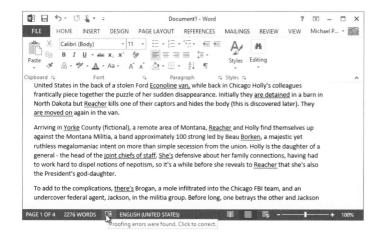

You may see blue, wavy underscores to indicate contextual spelling errors, where you misuse words, such as 'Their' in place of 'There'.

3 Proofing errors may be detected, as indicated by the wavy underscores – red (spelling) or blue (grammar and style)

4 Click the button on the status bar to correct them one by one, or correct them all at the same time when you've finished the document (see page 33)

Select and Copy Text

There are numerous ways provided in Word to select just the amount of text you need to work with, using the mouse or the keyboard, as preferred. To select the entire document, use one of these options:

1 Select the Home tab, click Select in the Editing group, and then click the Select All command

2 Move the mouse pointer to the left of any text until it turns into a right–pointing arrow, then triple-click to select all the text in the document

3 Press the shortcut keys Ctrl + A to select all the text

There are many mouse and keyboard options for selecting a piece of text in the body of the document. For example:

1 Double-click anywhere in a word to select it

2 Hold down Ctrl and click anywhere in a sentence to select the whole sentence

3 To select a portion of text, click at the start, hold down the left mouse button and drag the pointer over the required text, then release the button

30

...cont'd

You can use text selection in combination with the Clipboard tools, to copy or move multiple pieces of text in the same operation. For example:

1 Select the first section of required text using the mouse to highlight it

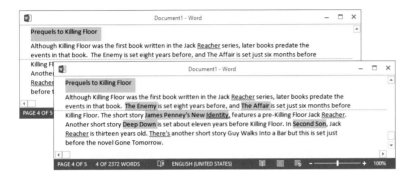

You can use the keyboard shortcuts
Ctrl + C (copy)
Ctrl + X (cut)
Ctrl + V (paste)
instead of the Clipboard buttons.

2 Hold down the Ctrl key and select additional pieces of text

3 Select Home and click the Copy button in the Clipboard group

Click the Cut button if you want to move the text rather than make a copy of it.

4 Click the position in the document where the text is required, then select Home and click the Paste button

Click the arrow below the Paste button to show Paste Options and choose between Keep Source Formatting, Merge Formatting, and Keep Text Only.

5 If you've copied several pieces of text, each piece appears on a separate line, so you will need to delete the end-of-line characters to join them up

31

Save the Document

When you are building a document, Word will periodically save a copy of the document, just in case a problem arises. This minimizes the amount of text you may need to re-enter. This feature is known as AutoRecover. To check the settings:

1 Click the File tab, select the Word Options and click the Save command

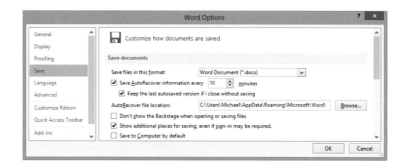

By default, Word will save AutoRecover information every 10 minutes, but you can change the frequency.

To make an immediate save of your document:

1 Click the Save button on the Quick Access toolbar

2 The first time, you are asked to confirm the location, the file name, and the document type that you want

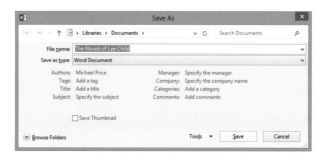

3 On subsequent saves, the document on the hard disk will be updated without further interaction

Beware

If the system terminates abnormally, any data entered since the last AutoRecover operation will be lost.

Don't forget

You can also select File, Save As, to specify a new location, name, or document type.

Correct Proofing Errors

When you've entered all the text, correct proofing errors.

1 Go to the start of the document with Ctrl + Home, then select Review tab, Spelling & Grammar

2 For terms or proper names, select Ignore All or you can select Add to put them in your custom dictionary

3 For spelling errors, choose the correct word and then click Change (or Change All to correct all occurrences)

4 Grammar and style errors are less definitive; decide about each suggestion on its merits and Ignore, Change or Revise as appropriate

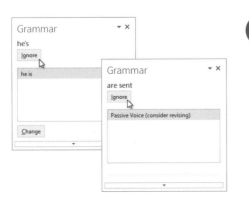

The proofing (i.e. spelling and grammar) check will commence from the current location of the typing cursor if you don't relocate to the start of the document.

Make sure that the appropriate spelling dictionary is enabled for the language of the document you are checking. See page 34.

Each error is presented in turn (unless previous choices, such as Ignore All, cause the error to get cleared), until the spelling check is completed.

Change Proofing Settings

You can make changes to the settings for the spelling checks, and for the grammar and style checks.

1 Select the File tab, then Word Options and Proofing

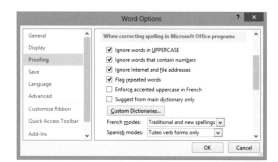

2 Settings, such as Ignore words in uppercase and Flag repeated words, apply to all Office applications

If you'd rather not use the grammar checker, clear the boxes for Mark grammar errors as you type and Check grammar with spelling. Alternatively, you can hide errors in that particular document.

3 Some proofing options are specific to an application, e.g. Word's Mark grammar errors as you type

4 Some options are specific to the document being edited

The suggestions that are offered for these examples of contextual errors are:

seen →

see →

Where or Here →

5 The spell checker in Word is contextual, identifying words that are spelled correctly but used inappropriately

Apply Styles

1 Select the Home tab then click in the main heading and select the style for Heading 1

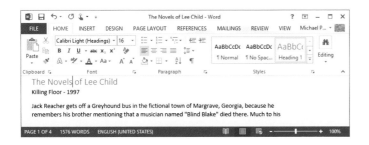

2 Click inside one of the subsidiary headings and select the style for Heading 2

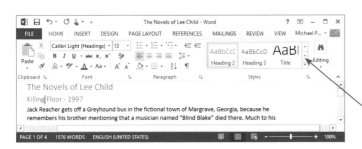

3 Click within one of the text paragraphs and select style for No Spacing

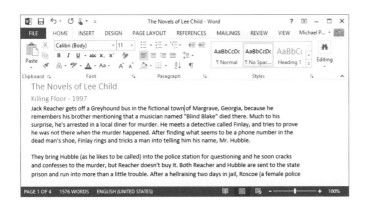

The spacing changes from the normal 1.5 lines to 1 line.

You can change the style for parts of the text to suit the particular contents, using the Styles group on the Home tab.

Click the down arrow to show the next row of styles.

Apply these two styles to other headings and paragraphs. To repeat a style, select an example, double-click the Format Painter icon, and then click each similar item in turn.

Outline View

When you have structured the document using headings, you can view it as an outline:

1 Select the View tab and click the Outline button, to switch to Outline view and enable the Outlining tab

You can also click the Outline button on the status bar, to switch to the hierarchical view.

2 In the Outline Tools group, click the box labeled Show First Line Only, to see more entries at once

Click the box Show Text Formatting to clear it. This displays the entries in plain text, to further increase the number of entries that can be shown.

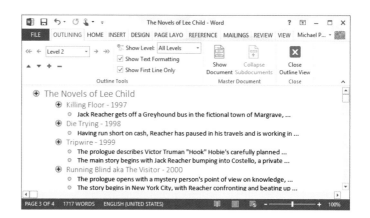

This makes it easier for you to review the whole document. You might decide that you want to try a different sequence, for example chronological order of events rather than date of publication. Outline view makes it easy to reposition entries.

...cont'd

1 Click the arrow next to Show Level, and choose Level 2

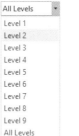

2 Locate an entry to move, e.g. The Enemy which precedes Killing Floor in date of action

This will display the selected level, and all the higher levels in the Outline of the document.

3 Click the Up arrow and the selected entry, with all its subsidiary levels and text, will move one row for each click on the arrow button

The Outline tools also provide buttons that allow you to promote or demote selected entries.

4 Repeat to reposition another entry, e.g. The Affair

You can click the + symbol next to an entry to select it, and then drag it to the required location.

5 Click the Down arrow to move a lower entry

Insert a Picture

1 Position the typing cursor at the location where the item is required, inserting a blank line if desired

You can insert a variety of items into your document, including pictures, tables, headers and footers, WordArt, and symbols.

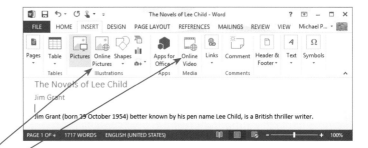

With Word 2013, you can also insert online pictures and video directly without having to download and save them on your computer.

2 Select the Insert tab and click the appropriate icon or command, for example Picture from Illustrations

The picture will be added to the document, in line with the text. Note the addition of the Picture Tools Format tab.

3 Locate the file for the picture, and click Insert

...cont'd

You can adjust the position of the picture on the text page.

1 Click the Position button in the Arrangements group and move the pointer over the buttons

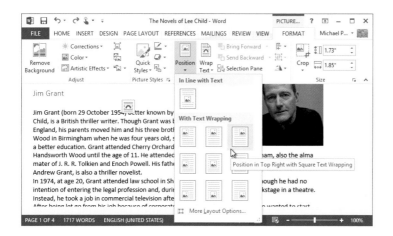

2 A live preview will be displayed. Click the appropriate button for the position you prefer

2 A live preview will be displayed. Click the appropriate button for the position you prefer

3 Click the up or down arrow on the height, to adjust the size of the picture proportionally

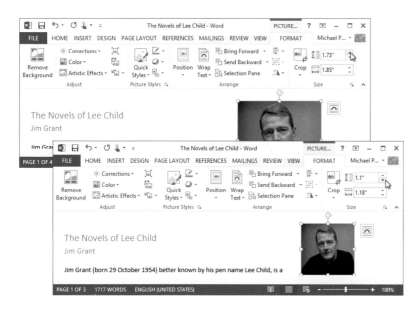

The Format tab allows you to change the size, select a frame, and adjust brightness, contrast, and color for the picture.

Having chosen the layout, you can select the picture to drag it and make fine adjustments.

The original proportions of the picture will be maintained, when you make changes to the height or width.

Page Layout

The Page Layout tab allows you to control how the document contents are placed on the page, by clicking one of the function command buttons in the Page Setup group.

1 Click the Orientation button to select Portrait or Landscape

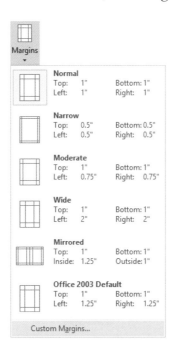

2 Click the Size button to select the paper size from the list, or click More Paper Sizes... to show other choices, including Custom Size

3 Click Margins to choose one of the predefined setups, e.g. Narrow, or click Custom Margins... to display the Page Setup dialog, and then enter the specific values

Display in Columns

1 Select the text to put into columns, click the Page Layout tab then select Columns from Page Setup

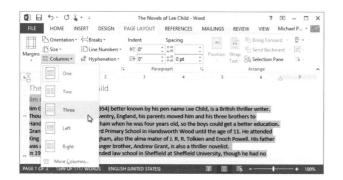

Hot tip

Leave all of the text unselected if you wish to apply the columns to the whole document.

2 Choose the number of columns required

Hot tip

Choose Justify for the paragraph text, to help give the document the appearance of newspaper columns. Choose Center, for the title text to place it over the three columns.

3 Click in the body text, click Home, Select, Select Text with Similar Formatting, and then click Justify

Don't forget

Select File, Options, Advanced, and choose to Keep track of formatting, to enable Select text with Similar Formatting.

Word Count

If you are preparing a document for a publication, such as a club magazine, you'll need to manage the number of words:

When there is text selected, the status bar shows word counts for the selection and the whole document.

97 OF 1717 WORDS

You can also display the word count details by selecting the Review tab and clicking Word Count, from Proofing.

1 View the word count for the document on the status bar

2 Click the word count for details, i.e. pages, paragraphs, lines and characters

For a fuller analysis of the contents of the document:

1 Select File, Options, Proofing, then Show readability statistics

2 Select the Review tab, then click Spelling & Grammar from the Proofing group and check the document

3 After the spelling check is completed, the document statistics are displayed

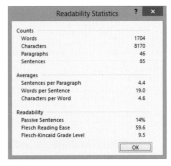

Create a Table

To specify a table in your document:

1 Click the point where you want the table, then click the Insert tab, and select Table

Hot tip

You'll see previews of the indicated table sizes as you move the pointer across the Insert Table area.

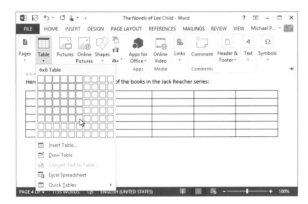

2 Move the pointer over the Insert Table area to select the number of rows and columns. Click to confirm

3 Type the contents, pressing Tab to move switch cells

Don't forget

Press the arrow keys to navigate around the table. Click and drag a separator line to adjust the width of a column.

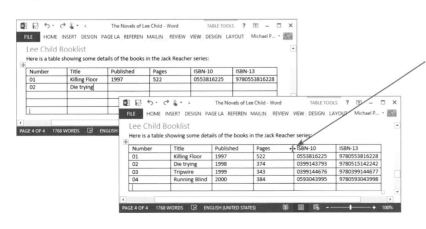

Convert Text to Table

If you already have the text for the table, perhaps taken from another document, you can convert the text into a table.

1 Make sure that the cell entries are separated by a comma or tab mark, or some other unique character

Select Home, then click the Show/ Hide button in the Paragraph group to display tabs and paragraph marks. Two consecutive commas or tabs indicate an empty cell. Paragraph marks separate rows.

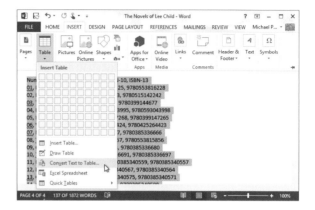

Select Autofit to contents, to adjust the column widths to match the data in those cells.

2 Highlight the text, select the Insert tab, and then click Table, Convert Text to Table

3 Specify your separation character and then click OK

4 The table will be created with the data inserted into the relevant cells, which may expand to hold the data

The cursor must be in the table area to display the Table Tools tab. Select Layout to apply operations, such as insert, delete, merge, and align.

Lee Child Booklist

Here is a table showing some details of the books in the Jack Reacher series:

Number	Title	Published	Pages	IDBN-10	ISBN-13
01	Killing Floor	1997	522	0553816225	9780553816228
02	Die Trying	1998	374	0399143793	9780515142242
03	Tripwire	1999	343	0399144676	9780399144677
04	Running Blind	2000	384	0593043995	9780593043998
05	Echo Burning	2001	384	0399147268	9780399147265
06	Without Fail	2002	374	0425264424	9780425264423
07	Persuader	2003	352	0385336667	9780385336666
08	The Enemy	2004	400	0553815857	9780553815856
09	One Shot	2005	384	0385336683	9780385336680
10	The Hard Way	2006	384	0385336691	9780385336697
11	Bad Luck and Trouble	2007	384	0385340559	9780385340557
12	Nothing to Lose	2008	416	0385340567	9780385340564
13	Gone Tomorrow	2009	432	0385340575	9780385340571

Paste Special

To copy the text without including formatting and graphics:

1 Highlight the text you want, then right-click the selected area and click the Copy command

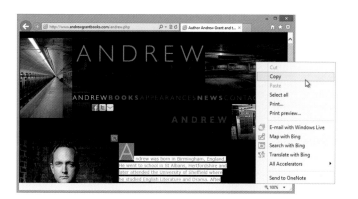

2 Click in the document where the text is needed, and on the Home tab, click the arrow below Paste

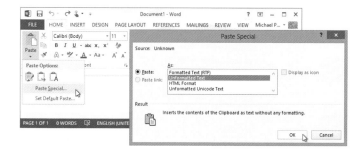

3 Click Paste Special and Paste, Unformatted Text

Hot tip

When you copy information from other documents, or from web pages, the text may include graphics, formatting, and colors that are inappropriate for your document.

Beware

Graphical information won't be copied, even if it has the appearance of text (as with the initial A for Andrew in the text being copied for this example).

Don't forget

The copied text will inherit the format of that part of the document you clicked before carrying out the paste operation.

Print Document

1 To print your document from within Word, click the File tab and select Print (or press Ctrl + P)

In Office 2013 programs, you can preview and print your documents at one location – in the Print section of the BackStage.

You can view the document as it will appear in print by selecting the View tab and selecting the Print Layout button from the View group.

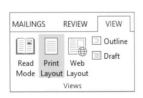

2 Here, you can preview the document, using the zoom slider, the scroll bars, and the page change buttons

3 Select the specific printer to use

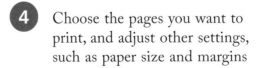

4 Choose the pages you want to print, and adjust other settings, such as paper size and margins

5 Specify the number of copies, then click the Print button

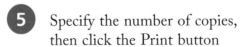

Quick Print
You can add the Quick Print button to the Quick Access Toolbar (see page 16), to print the current document, using the default settings.

3 Complex Documents

Microsoft Word can be used to create and edit complex documents, such as booklets and brochures. This chapter covers import text, insert illustrations, and create tables of contents and illustrations, and shows how templates can be used. It also introduces Publisher, the Office application specifically designed for desktop publishing.

Start a Booklet

To illustrate some of the facilities available for creating and organizing complex documents, we'll go through the process of importing and structuring the text for a booklet based on *A Study in Scarlet* by Sir Arthur Conan Doyle.

1 To start, type the book title, author, and chapter titles

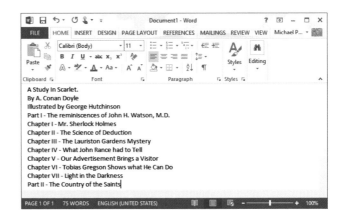

48

2 When you've entered these details, set the language. This is a United Kingdom book, so press Ctrl + A to highlight text, select Review, Language, Set Proofing Language, English (United Kingdom) and click OK

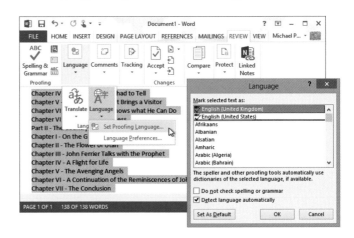

3 Click Save on the Quick Access toolbar, and type a document name (or accept the suggested name)

Choose Page Arrangement

Now specify the paper size, the margins and the page style.

1 Select the Page Layout tab, and click Size to choose the paper size you are printing on, e.g. Letter

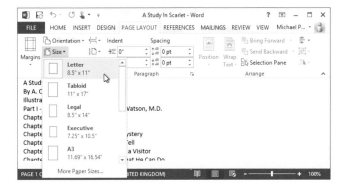

Similarly, you can click Margins to select the size you want to use, for example Normal.

2 Click the down arrow on Page Setup group to show the associated dalog

3 In Pages, select Multiple pages, Book fold

4 Specify the number of sheets per booklet

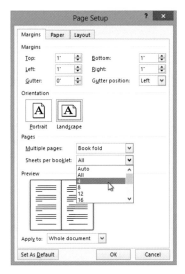

The orientation changes to landscape, and you get four pages of the document on each piece of paper (printed on both sides). A four-sheet booklet, for example, would be printed as:

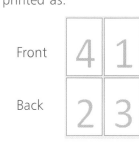

You specify the number of sheets in multiples of 4 up to 40, to assemble the document in blocks of pages or choose All to assemble as a single booklet.

Create the Structure

1 Highlight the text for the chapter titles

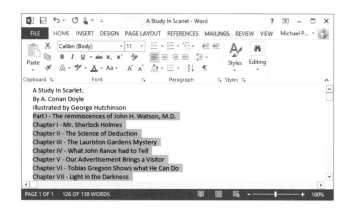

Hot tip

This particular book has two parts, with seven chapters in each part.

Don't forget

The formatting changes center the chapter titles over the text that will be inserted (see page 52).

2 Click Home and select Quick Styles, Heading 1

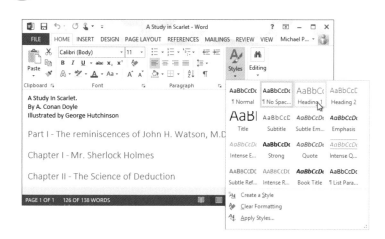

Hot tip

Steps 4 to 6 illustrate how you can use Find and Replace to insert special characters, such as line breaks.

3 With the chapter titles still selected, click the Center button in the Paragraph group

4 To replace hyphens with line breaks in the chapter titles, click the Editing button and select Replace, again with the text for the chapter titles selected

5 In the Find what box, type a hyphen, with a space either side, that is " - " (without the quotation marks)

You can use Alt + FS shortcut keys to activate the Find and Replace box at any time and this works for other applications too.

6 In the Replace with box, type "^l" (the control code for a manual line break), then select Replace All

You can click the More button and select Special, Manual Line Break, to insert the required code.

7 This changes all the occurrences in the selected text. Click No to skip the remainder of the document, to avoid changing hyphens elsewhere in the text

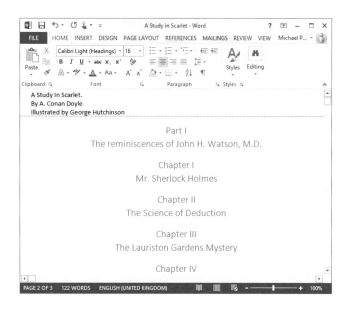

To see the paragraph and line-break codes, click the Show/ Hide button (in the Paragraph group on the Home tab).

Note that each title remains a single item, even though spread over two lines.

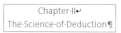

Import Text

1 Click to the left of the Chapter I title, select Insert, Page Break, and so start the chapter on a new page

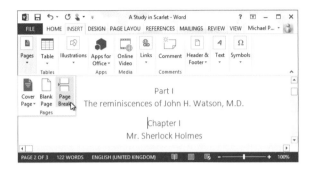

Hot tip

Type paragraphs of text, insert text from a file, or copy and paste text from a file, if you just want part of the contents.

2 Click the page, just past the end of the title, and press Enter to add a blank line (in Body Text style)

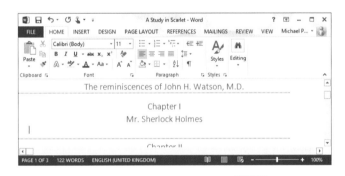

Don't forget

This option was known as Insert File in previous versions of Word. It allows you to transfer the contents from various file types, including Word, web, and text.

3 Select Insert, Insert Object, and choose Text from File

4 Go to the folder and file for the chapter text

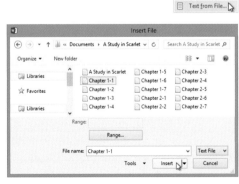

5 Click Insert to add the text

...cont'd

6 Click OK to select the appropriate encoding, if prompted

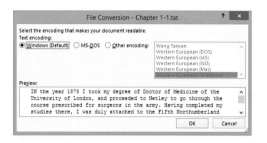

Hot tip

Step 6 is only required when the system needs your help in interpreting the imported text.

The text is copied to the document at the required location.

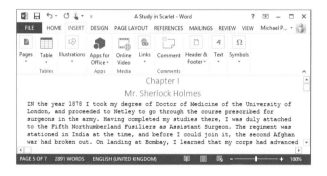

Repeat steps 1 to 5 for each chapter in the book.

To adjust the style for the inserted text:

1 Click anywhere in the new text, click the Home tab, then click Select and choose Select Text with Similar Formatting

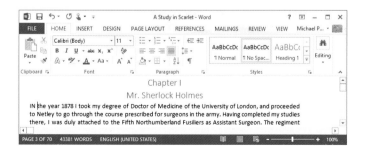

Hot tip

The inserted text may not have the format you require, but you can change all the inserted text in a single operation to a style that you prefer.

2 Select your preferred style, e.g. Normal, No Spacing, plus Justify and the inserted text will be converted

Insert Illustrations

The sample text has the titles for the illustrations at the required locations, in the form of: Figure: Title of illustration.

1 Find the location for an illustration. For example, select Home, click Find, and search for Figure:

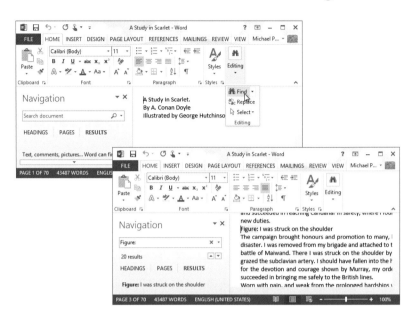

You can insert pictures from image files of all the usual types, including bitmap, JPEG (photos), and GIF (web graphics).

2 At the location, select Insert and click Picture

3 Locate the file containing the required illustration and click Insert, and the picture is inserted into the document, in line with the text

4 Adjust its size and position as required

Add Captions

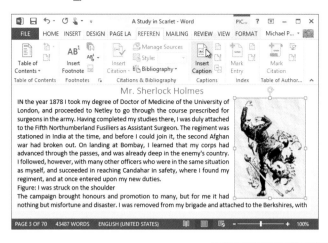

Repeat these two sets of steps to insert a picture and a caption for each of the figures in the book.

① Select Reference, Insert Caption and click OK

② Click OK to accept the automatic number

If the document doesn't already contain the title for the illustration, type it after the automatic number in the Caption box, or in the document itself after Figure #.

Figure 1

Figure 1: I was struck

Figure 1: I was struck

③ Type a colon and a space, then copy or type the text for the picture title to follow after the figure number

④ Click away from the caption to see the figure as it will appear in the final document

⑤ Repeat this procedure for each of the pictures in the document, until you have all the figures and captions

The captions you enter are used to build a table of illustrations (see page 58).

Table of Contents

When you have formatted heading levels in the document, you can use these to create and maintain a contents list.

1 Select Home, Find, Go To, then select Page and type 2, then click Go To and Close, to show that page

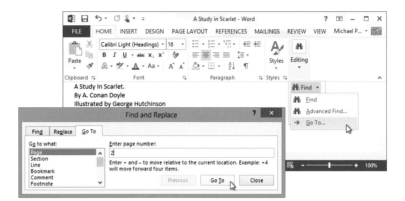

2 Select the Insert tab and click Blank Page in the Pages group, to insert a page for the contents list

3 Go to the new page 2, select the References tab, and click the Table of Contents button

4 Choose the type of table that you want, for example Automatic Table 1 (with Contents as the title)

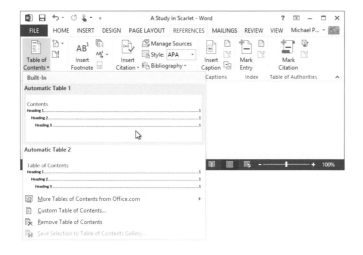

5 The table of contents is inserted into the document

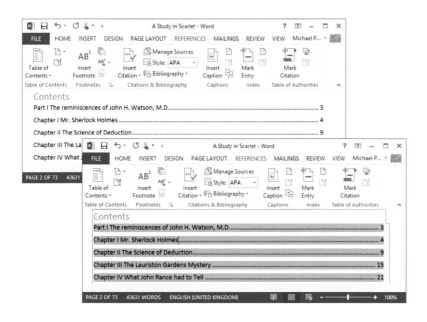

6 When you click in the table of contents, its entries are grayed, to indicate field codes (action items)

Table of Illustrations

1 Go to the start of chapter 1 of your document and insert another blank page, this time for a list of illustrations

2 On the new page, type Illustrations, select the Home tab, the arrow to expand Style, and pick Heading 1

3 Press Enter to add a blank line, click References and click the button for Table of Figures Dialog

4 Select the Caption label, i.e. Figures, then select or clear the boxes to Show page numbers, Right align page numbers and Include label and number

Don't forget

Entries for the chosen caption type, in this case Figures, will be identified and included in the table.

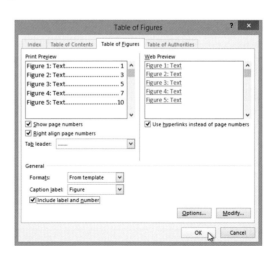

5 Click OK to insert the table of figures as shown in the Print Preview

...cont'd

6   The layout for the table of figures is similar to that of the table of contents created previously

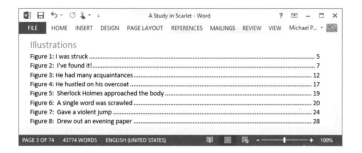

There's no heading included, so any heading required must be provided separately, in this case, Illustrations.

7   Click the table to see the grayed entries indicating that there are field codes and links to the figures

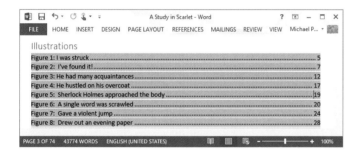

8   Highlight the table and select Toggle Field Codes

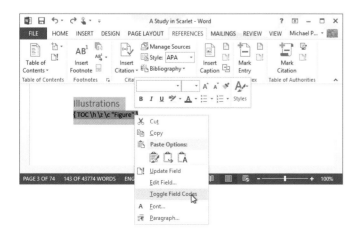

The format of the field code for the table of figures indicates that it is actually a TOC (table of contents) based on the Figure label.

Insert Preface

1 Go to page 2 (the contents page) and insert a blank page for the book preface

2 On the new page, type Preface, select the Home tab, the arrow to expand the Styles group, and Heading 2

If you want the preface to appear on an odd-numbered (right-hand) page, insert a second blank page in front of it.

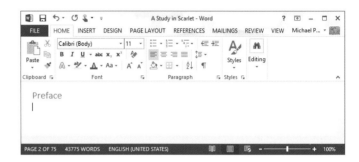

3 Press Enter and insert text from a file (see page 52), or type the text for the preface

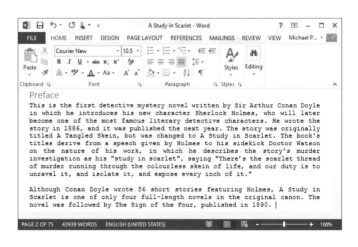

Save the document whenever you make substantial changes, to avoid the risk of losing your updates.

4 Adjust the formatting and alignment of the text as desired, for example selecting Justify for the main portion

5 Select Save on the Quick Access toolbar to save the latest changes that you have made

Update Table of Contents

When you make changes, such as to the preface or the illustrations list, that include new headings (level 1, 2 or 3), the table of contents is affected. However, the updates will not be displayed immediately. To apply the updates:

1 Locate the table of contents and click within it

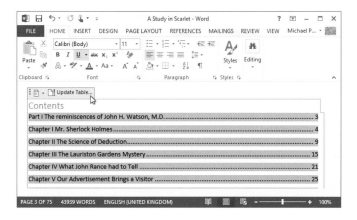

2 Select Update entire table to add new items to the table and click OK

3 New entries are inserted and the page numbers are updated as appropriate

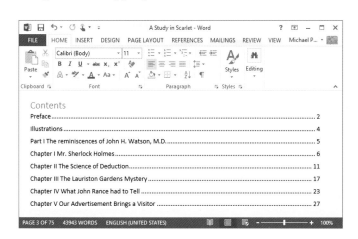

Hot tip

Whenever you add text to the document, or insert pages, the page numbers for the entries in the table of contents change, but the changes will not appear until you explicitly select Update Table.

Don't forget

If you've added pages or text to your document, but have not changed the headings, you can select Update page numbers only.

61

Decorate the Page

Hot tip

Finally, you can enhance the formatting of the title page, using styles or WordArt.

1 Select a section of text, click Styles, and move the mouse over the options presented to preview styles

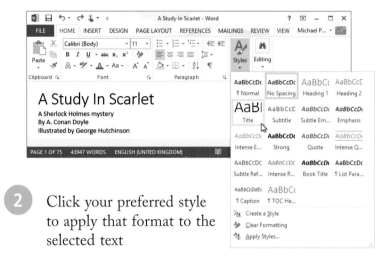

2 Click your preferred style to apply that format to the selected text

3 For example, select the book title and choose the Title style. For other selections of text you can pick styles such as Subtitle or an Emphasis option

Title, centered

Subtitle, centered

Intense Emphasis

Emphasis, centered

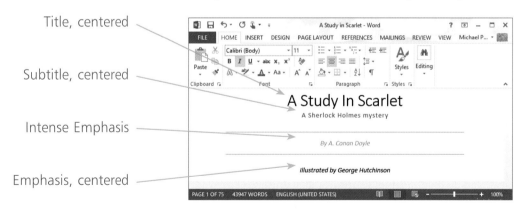

4 Select Center if desired. Some styles, e.g. Intense Emphasis, are centered by default

5 For more impact select text and choose WordArt from the Insert tab, Text group

...cont'd

6 Review the WordArt styles and select an option

The WordArt effects are not displayed during Insert until you select a specific option. You can select a different option, or clear the WordArt if you change your mind.

7 The text is displayed in the selected style and color

8 Explore WordArt Styles, including Text Fill, Text Outline and Text Effects, and apply preferred options

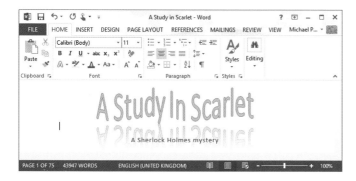

This illustrates the Full Reflection and Double Wave Transform, two of the options offered in the Text Effects.

Templates

1 Click the File tab, select New, and scroll through the featured templates to find one that meets your needs

When you need a specialized form of document, you can use a predefined template document to help you get started.

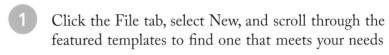

2 If there's nothing appropriate shown, look online for templates, for example search for greetings cards

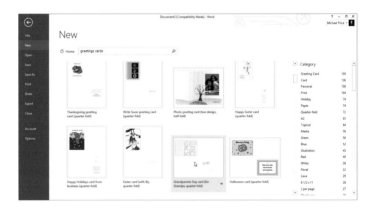

When you carry out a search, you will see a list of around 100 template categories, with counts of the number of templates in each category. Use this list to refine your searches.

3 Select the desired template, and click the Create button to download the template and open a new document based on that template

4 The template file is downloaded to your computer and saved on your hard disk

When you download a template, it is added to the list of featured templates, so it is easy to find if you need to access it in future.

5 When the transfer completes, the new document based on the downloaded template will be opened

This template is a four fold document and part of the content is inverted, so that it appears correctly when folded. Other templates may be two fold or single sheet.

6 Change the contents of the text box to personalize the document, or delete the text to leave space for a handwritten message

7 Print the document, or Save it with an appropriate file name to work with it at a later time

Note that Templates in the older Word formats open documents in Compatibility Mode (see page 25). The document can be upgraded to the latest format when saved.

Publisher

Publisher provides a higher level of desktop publishing capability, with a great variety of paper sizes and styles, including many templates for brochures and leaflets, etc.

Publisher is included in the Professional editions of Office 2013 and in all the Office 365 editions.

1 Start the Publisher application, which opens with the Start screen and a selection of document templates

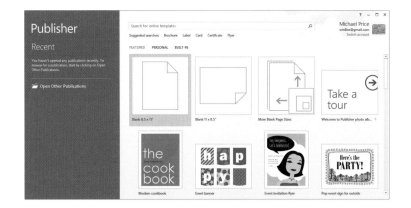

2 Explore the templates offered or search for online templates by topic, for example birthday

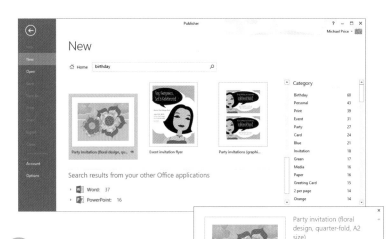

You can scroll through the images for a template with multiple pages. Click the [X] Close button to return to the list.

3 Review the selection provided, and select any template to see an enlarged version, and details of its format

Create a Publication

1 Choose a template, such as Party invitation and click the Create button

2 The template will be downloaded and a new document based on that template is opened

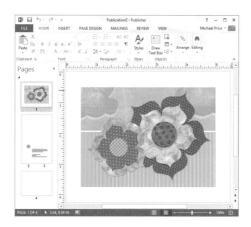

3 Click section 2 & 3 to see the middle sections

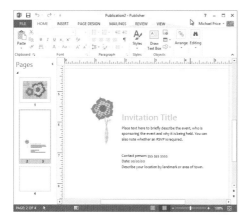

4 Enter the title and description for the invitation, along with contact and location details and Save

Don't forget

The greeting card is divided into four sections, each one-quarter of the physical page, making it easier to view and edit the parts of the card.

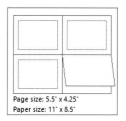

Page size: 5.5" x 4.25"
Paper size: 11" x 8.5"

Hot tip

Publisher offers various different sizes and layouts of greetings cards, for example:

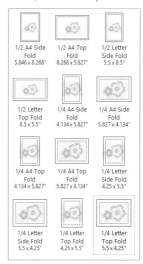

Print the Publication

Note that Publisher shows the pages in a horizontal upright format, but will adjust the orientation of each page when you are ready to print the document.

1 Select pages 2 and 4 to add text and images to those sections then save the final document

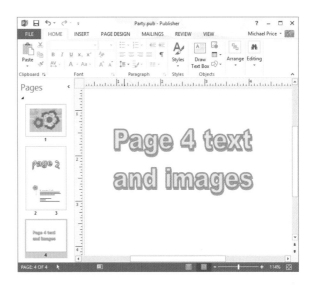

Don't forget

Once printed, the sheet is folded in half, and then folded in half again, to form the greeting card.

2 Select File, Print, to see the document as it prints, a single sheet, with sections 2, 3 and 4 inverted

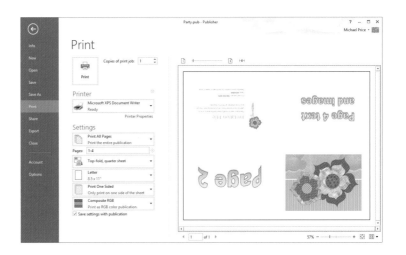

3 Adjust the settings as required, select the printer that you wish to use and then click the Print button

4 Calculations

This chapter looks at Excel, the spreadsheet application, in which you can create workbooks, enter data, replicate values, format numbers, add formulas and functions, and make use of templates.

Start Excel

To start Microsoft Excel 2013 with a fresh new spreadsheet using the temporary name Book1:

1 On the Start screen select the Excel tile, or on the Desktop select the Excel icon

Alternatively, right-click an empty part of a folder window; select New, Microsoft Office Excel Worksheet.

Double-click the file icon New Microsoft Office Excel Worksheet, to display and edit that document.

2 From the Excel Start screen select the Blank workbook to open a new spreadsheet called Book1

3 You will find that Excel opens immediately with the blank document Book1, if you have previously selected File, Excel Options, General and cleared the box Show Start screen when this application starts

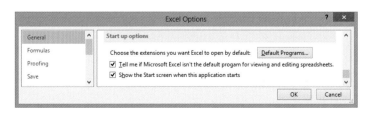

...cont'd

The spreadsheet presented is an Excel workbook that contains, initially, a single worksheet which is blank. The cells that it contains are empty – all 17 million of them.

1 To move to the last row (1048576) in the worksheet, press End, and then press the down arrow

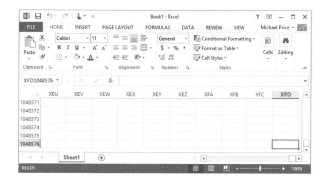

2 To move to the last column (XFD) in the worksheet, press End, and then press the right arrow

If the worksheet contains data, the action taken depends on the initial location of the selected cell.

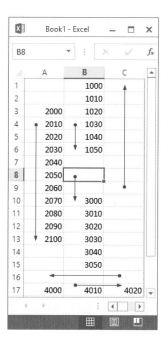

3 If the selected cell contains data, pressing End and then an arrow key goes to the edge of the data area

4 If the current cell is empty, you move to the start of the adjacent data area

5 If there's no more data in that direction, you'll move to the edge of the worksheet, as with an empty worksheet

There can be up to 1048576 rows and 16384 columns. This compares with 65536 rows and 256 columns in earlier releases.

It may be impractical to utilize even a fraction of the total number of cells available, but the enlarged sheet size does give greater flexibility in designing spreadsheets. For larger amounts of data, you should use Access (see page 106).

The movement is always in the direction of the arrow key that you select after pressing End.

Enter Data

The most common use of spreadsheets is for financial planning, for example to keep track of business and travel expenditure. To create a family budget:

1 Open a blank worksheet, select cell A1 and type the title for the spreadsheet, e.g. Family Budget

2 Press the Enter or down key to insert the text and move to cell A2, then type the next entry, Income

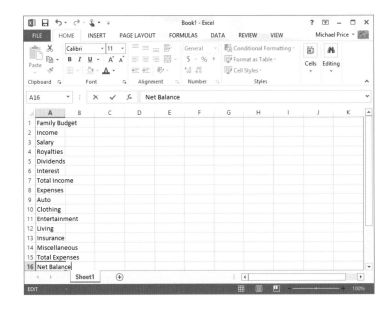

3 Repeat this process to add the remaining labels for the income and expense items you want to track, and labels for the totals and balance

...cont'd

If you omit an item, you can insert an additional worksheet row. For example, to include a second Salary income item:

1 Click a cell (e.g. C4) in the row just below where the new entry is required, and select Cells, Insert, Insert Sheet Rows from the Cells group on the Home tab

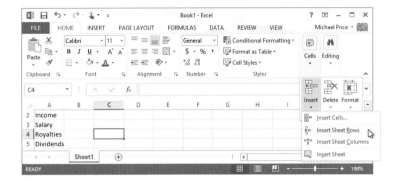

Hot tip

Select a vertical group of cells to insert that many rows above the selected cells. Note that you can insert one or more columns in a similar manner, by selecting Insert, Insert Sheet Columns.

2 Enter the additional label, e.g. "Salary 2nd", in A4

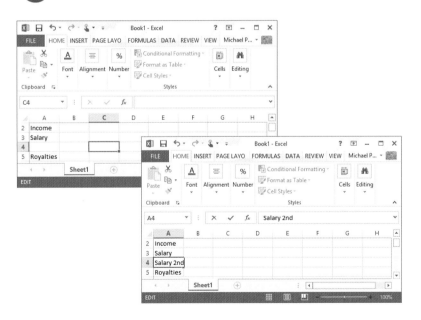

Don't forget

You can also select the cell and press F2, or click anywhere on the formula bar, to make changes to the content of a cell.

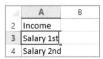

3 Double-click an existing cell to edit or retype the entry, e.g. to change "Salary" to "Salary 1st" in A3

Quick Fill

You can create one column of data, then let Excel replicate the cell contents for you. For example:

1 Enter month and values in column C, January in C2 and values in cells C3-C7 and C10-C15

Don't forget

You can widen column A to accommodate the whole text (see page 80), then delete column B.

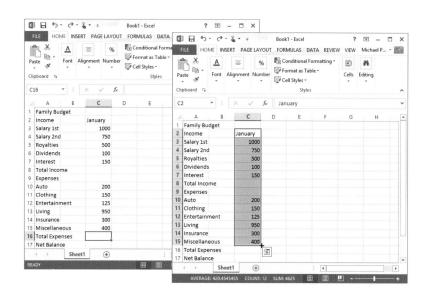

Hot tip

Click in cell C2, hold down the Shift key and click in cell C15 to highlight the whole range of cells.

2 Highlight cells C2-C15, move the mouse pointer over the box at the bottom right, and, when it becomes a **+,** drag it to the right to replicate the cells

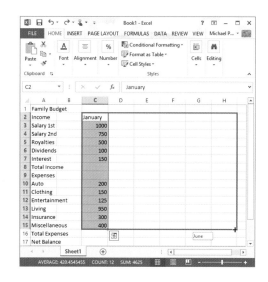

...cont'd

3 Release the mouse pointer when the required number of columns is indicated

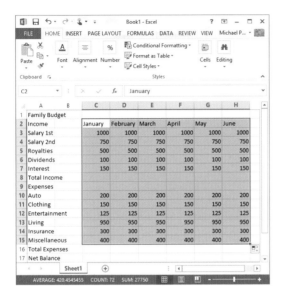

4 Numeric values are duplicated, but the month name is detected and the succeeding months are inserted

After you've used the Fill handle, the Auto Fill Options button appears. Click this to control the action, for example to replicate the formatting only, or to copy cells without devising a series such as Months.

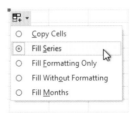

5 As you enter data into the worksheet, remember to periodically click the Save button

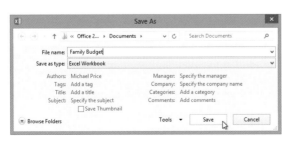

75

Sums and Differences

When you've entered the data, and made the changes required, you can introduce functions and formulas to complete the worksheet.

1 Click cell C8 (total income for January), then select the Home tab and click Editing and then AutoSum to sum the adjacent values

Don't forget

The numerical cells in a block immediately adjacent to the selected cell will be selected, and included in the AutoSum function. Always check that Excel has selected the appropriate cells.

2 Press Enter to show the total, then repeat the procedure for cell C16 (total expenses for January)

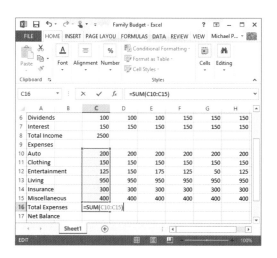

3 Click in cell C17 (the cell reserved for the net balance for the month of January)

...cont'd

4 Type =, click C8, type -, and then click C16 (to calculate total income minus total expenses for Jan.)

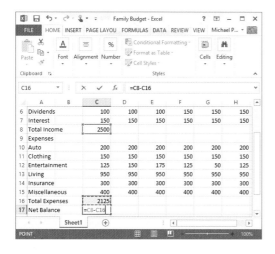

Hot tip

The = symbol indicates that the following text is a formula. You can type the cell references, or click on the cell itself, and Excel will enter the appropriate reference.

5 Press Enter to add the formula and display the result

6 Select cell C8 and use the Fill handle to replicate the formula for the other months (e.g. February to June), and repeat this process for cells C16 and C17

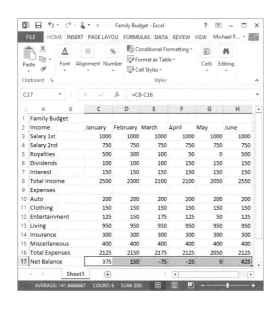

Don't forget

When the formula is replicated, the cell references, e.g. C8:C16, are incremented, to D8:D16, E8:E16 etc.

Formatting

78

1 Click A1 (the title cell), then select the Home tab, choose a larger font size, and a font effect, e.g. Bold

Hot tip

Changing the format for various parts of the worksheet can make it easier to review and assess the results.

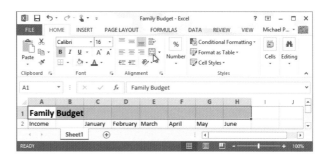

2 Press Shift, and click H1 to highlight the row across the data, then click the Merge and Center button

Don't forget

You can change each cell individually, or press Ctrl and click each of the cells to select them, then apply the changes to all the cells at once.

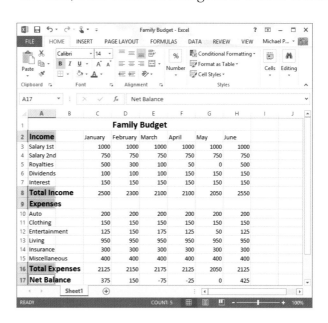

3 Click the Categories and Totals labels (e.g. A2, A8, A9, A16, A17), and change the font size and effects

4 Alternatively, click Cell Styles to pick a suitable style

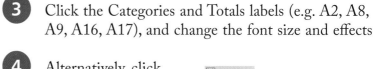

To emphasize the "Net Balance" values for each month:

1 Select the range of cells, e.g. C17:H17

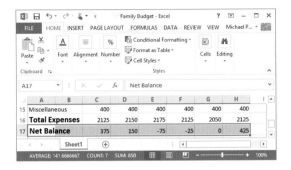

2 Select Styles, Conditional Formatting, Color Scales to choose a color scale, e.g. Green–Yellow–Red

3 The cells are colored and shaded appropriately for the values that they contain

Rounding Up

You can use Excel functions, such as Round Up or Ceiling, to adjust the solutions of numerical problems, such as the number of tiles needed to cover the floor area of a room.

1 Open a new, blank worksheet, and enter these labels in the first column:

Number of Tiles
Tile Length
Tile Width
Room Length
Room Width
Number of Tiles
Per Box
Boxes

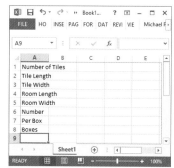

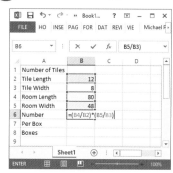
2 Enter sample sizes in cells B2:B5, making sure that you use the same units for tile and room dimensions

3 In cell B6, type the formula =(B4/B2)*(B5/B3)

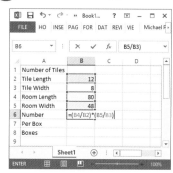 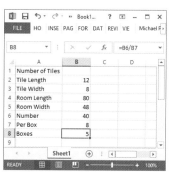

4 In cell B8, type the formula =B6/B7

On the basis of this result, you might think 5 boxes would be sufficient. However, if you fit the tiles to the area, you find some tiles have to be trimmed. while part of the area is left uncovered.

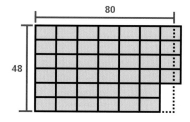

...cont'd

To ensure that there are enough whole tiles to completely cover the area, you need to round up the evaluations:

1 Copy B2:B8 to C2:C8, and, in cell C6, type the formula =CEILING(B4/B2,1)*CEILING(B5/B3,1)

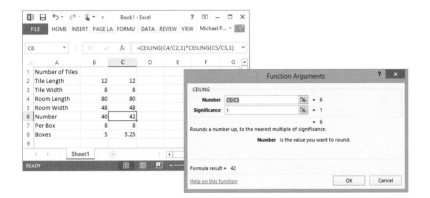

The CEILING function rounds the results up to the next significant value, in this case, the next highest integer. If the tiles have a repeat pattern, you might need to use the pattern size as the significant number.

The number of whole tiles increases to 42, which will now cover the complete floor area, even after cutting.

This gives 5.25 boxes. If boxes must be purchased in whole numbers, this result also needs rounding up.

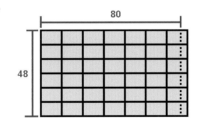

2 Copy C2:C8 to D2:D8, and, in cell D8, type the formula =ROUNDUP(D6/D7,0) to get the result: 6 boxes needed

The ROUNDUP function is another way to adjust values. Here it is used to round up the result to zero decimal places, which also gives the next highest integer.

Find a Function

There are a large number of functions available in Excel, they are organized into a library of groups to make it easier to find the one you need.

1 Select the Formulas tab to show Function Library

Hot tip

Clicking the More Functions button will display a secondary list of categories.

2 Click a category in Function Library, for an alphabetical list of its functions

3 If you don't know where to search for the function you want, click the Insert Function button

Don't forget

You can also click the Insert Function button on the formula bar.

4 Choose a category, e.g. Financial, and pick a function from the list offered

Hot tip

Enter keywords related to the activity you want to perform, and Excel will list all potentially relevant functions.

5 Alternatively, type a description and click Go, then select one of the recommended functions

Don't forget

The function arguments for the selected function are shown, and a brief description is provided.

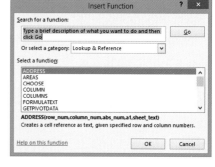

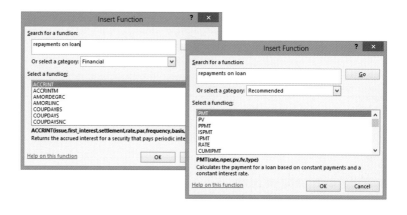

...cont'd

6 Select a suitable function, e.g. PMT, and click OK

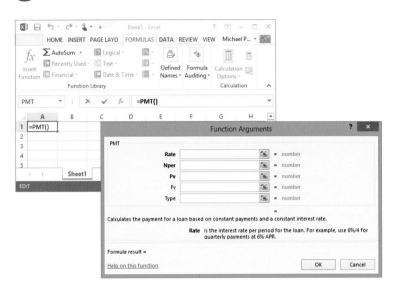

Don't forget

Rate is the interest rate for the payment interval (e.g. per month), Nper is the number of periods (e.g. number of months), and Pv is the present value (loan amount).

7 Type the values for the arguments (Rate, Nper, etc.), using the definition provided as you select each item

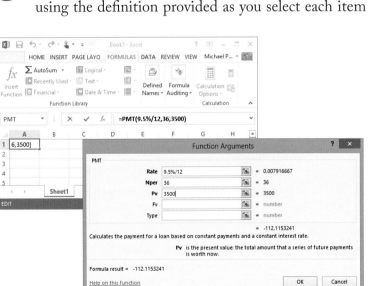

Hot tip

You can, optionally, provide a final value, Fv (the cash balance), and also specify the Type (payments made at the start or the end of each period).

8 The result is displayed (a negative figure, indicating a payment) and the function is inserted into the cell

Goal Seeking

Using the PMT function, you can establish the monthly payments required to pay off a long-term loan, e.g. 25 years.

To calculate payments for an interest-only loan, set Fv (see page 83) to the same value as the loan amount.

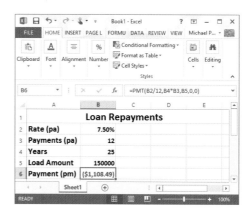

Suppose, however, you'd like to know how many years it will take to pay off the loan if you make payments of $1500.

1 One way to establish this is by trial and error, adjusting the number of years to get that payment

You would carry on refining your estimate, e.g. trying 12 then 14, to discover that the correct answer lies between these two periods.

2 Try 20 years, then 15 years, then 10 years, the payment then goes above $1500. So the appropriate period would be between 10 and 15 years

However, Excel provides an automatic way to apply this type of process, and this gives you an exact answer very quickly.

...cont'd

1 Click the cell containing the function, select the Data tab, and click What If Analysis in Data Tools

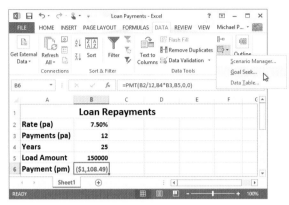

Hot tip

Use the Scenario Manager to create a set of results for a range of values, such as 10, 15 and 20 years of repayments.

2 Select the Goal Seek option and specify the required result -1500 (the payment per month) and the change to cell B4 (the number of years for full repayment)

3 Goal Seeking tries out various values for the changing cell, until the solution is found

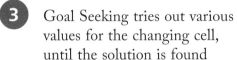

4 Click OK to see the revised results in the worksheet

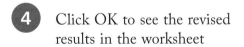

Beware

You must specify the target payment as a negative value, since it is a repayment, otherwise Goal Seeking will be unable to find a solution.

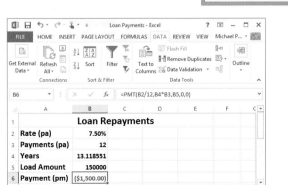

Templates

Hot tip

You can get started with your worksheet by using one of the ready-made templates, which are offered for many common requirements.

1 Select the File tab and click the New button

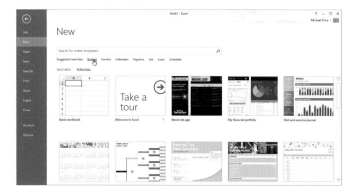

2 Select any template to view its content, and click Create to open a document using that template

3 Alternatively, select a category to review the templates from Microsoft Office Online

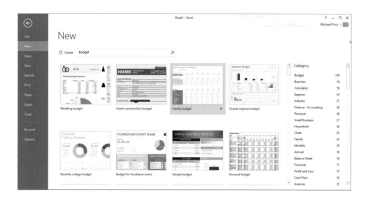

Don't forget

Check periodically to find out what new templates have been added to the Office Online website.

4 Choose a template to see the layout, and click Create to download the template and open a document based on that template

5 Manage Data

With Excel you can import data, apply sorts and filters, and select specific subsets. The data can be used to create a chart, or arranged in tables, where you can insert totals and computations and look up values. For full database management functions you'd use Access, included with some editions of Office.

Import Data

You won't have to type the information into your worksheets, if the data is already available in another application. For example, to import data from a delimited text file:

1 Click the File tab and select Open

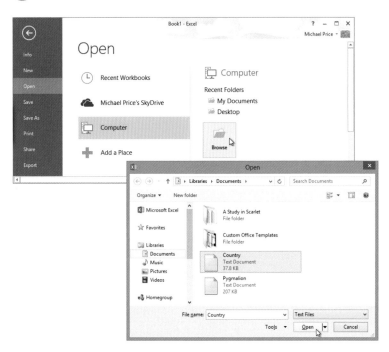

2 Select the file with the data you wish to import and click Open to start the Text Import Wizard, which recognizes the delimited file. Click Next to continue

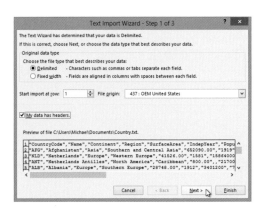

…cont'd

3 Choose the delimiter (e.g. Comma) and click Next

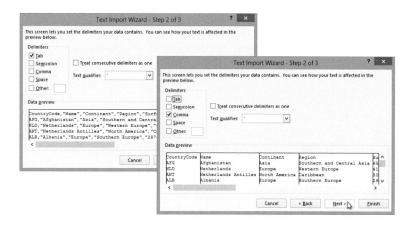

When you choose a delimiter, you can see the effect on the text in the preview area.

4 Adjust column formats, if required, then click Finish

The default format is General, which will handle most situations, but you can select specific data formats where appropriate.

5 The data is presented as an Excel worksheet

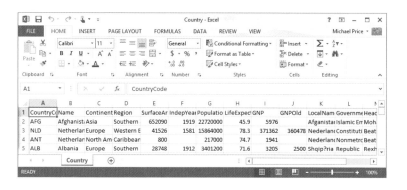

Explore the Data

Select the File tab, click Save As and choose file type Excel Workbook, to save the data as a standard Excel file.

1 Double-click or drag the separators between the columns to reveal more of the data they contain

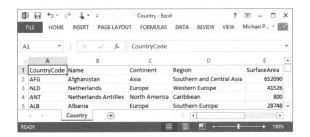

2 Select the View tab, click Freeze Panes in the Window group, and select Freeze Top Row

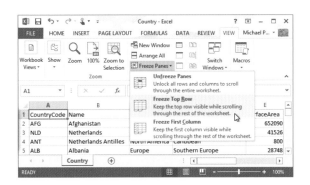

Freezing the top row makes the headings it contains visible, whichever part of the worksheet is being displayed.

3 Press Ctrl + End to move to the last cell in the data area and again adjust column widths as desired

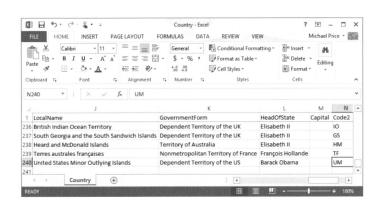

This will show you how many rows and columns there are in the data (in this example, 240 rows and 14 columns).

Sort

1 Click a cell in the Name column, select the Data tab and click A–Z (ascending) to sort by name

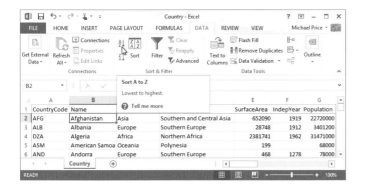

You can also select the Sort options from the Editing group on the Home tab.

2 Click a cell in the Population column and click Z–A (descending), to sort from highest to lowest

If you click in a single cell, Excel will select all the surrounding data and sort the rows of contiguous data into the required order.

3 To sort by more than one value, click the Sort button

You can sort the data into sequence using several levels of values.

...cont'd

If a selection of the worksheet is highlighted when you click one of the buttons, the sort may be restricted to the selected data.

For data organized by columns, rather than rows, click the Options button and select Sort left to right.

4 Click the arrow in the Sort by box and select the main sort value, for example, Continent

5 Click the Add Level button and select the additional sort values, for example, Region and then Population

6 Change the sort sequence, if needed, then click OK to sort by population within region and continent

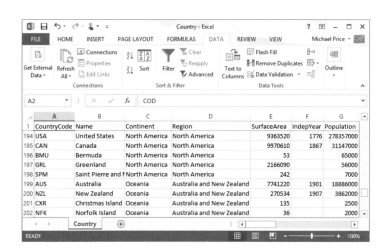

Filters

You can filter the data to hide entries that are not of immediate interest.

1 Click a cell within the data area, select the Data tab and click Filter in the Sort & Filter group

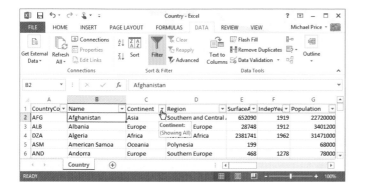

Hot tip

You can also select the Filter button from within the Editing group on the Home tab (see page 91).

2 Click a filter icon, e.g. Continent, to display its AutoFilter

3 Click the Select All box, to deselect all entries, then select the specific entry you want, e.g. Oceania

4 Click OK to apply the filter

Hot tip

Filtering is turned on, and a filter icon (an arrow) is added to each heading, with an initial setting of Showing All.

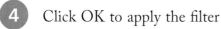

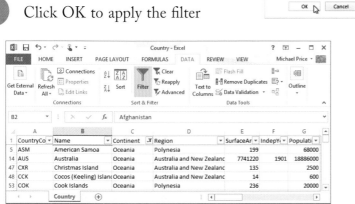

Number Filters

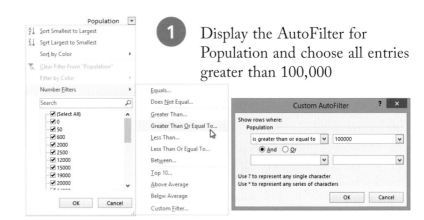

You can set number filters, where you specify a level at which to accept or reject entries, or choose an option, e.g. accepting the top 10 entries.

1 Display the AutoFilter for Population and choose all entries greater than 100,000

2 The filter icons for modified AutoFilters are changed, to show that filtering is in effect for those columns

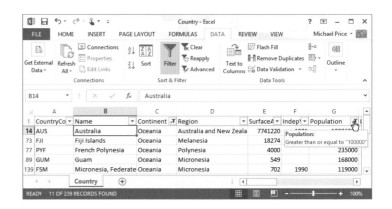

If you click the Filter button on the Data tab, or the Home tab, it will remove all the filters and delete all the filter settings.

Filter

3 Click a filter icon and select the Clear Filter option, to remove the filter for a particular column

4 The filter icon for that column reverts to an arrow, and the Showing All option is applied

Select Specific Data

Suppose you want to examine the population values for the larger countries. You can hide away information that's not relevant for that purpose:

1 Use the AutoFilter on the Population column, to display only countries whose populations are greater than 150 million

Hot tip

Filter the rows and hide selected columns to remove the data not needed at the moment from view.

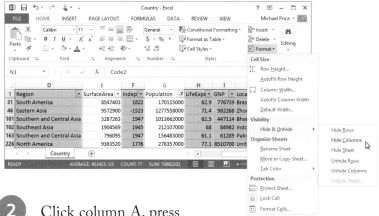

2 Click column A, press Ctrl, click columns C, D, etc. and select Home, Format, Hide & Unhide, Hide Columns

3 The remaining data is displayed, and you can sort this if desired

Don't forget

This places the column of country names adjacent to the columns of surface area and population values, ready for further analysis, creating a chart for example. To help with this, you can sort the information, e.g. in descending order of population size.

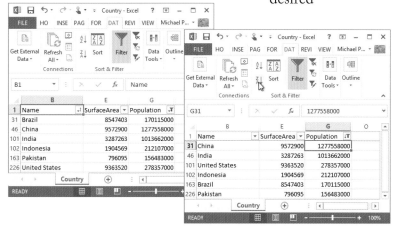

Create a Chart

1 Highlight the data (including headers), select the Insert tab and click the arrow on the Charts group

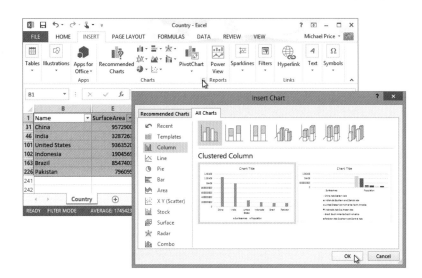

Hot tip

When you've created a chart, the Chart Tools Design and Format tabs are displayed, and you can select the Change Chart Type button to try one of the other options.

2 Choose the chart type and subtype, in this case, Column and Clustered Column

Beware

The Surface Area values are numerically much smaller than the Population values, so are very close to the horizontal axis and almost invisible. However, you can choose a secondary axis for the population values to make both sets of values visible.

3 Click a Population column and select Format Data Series...

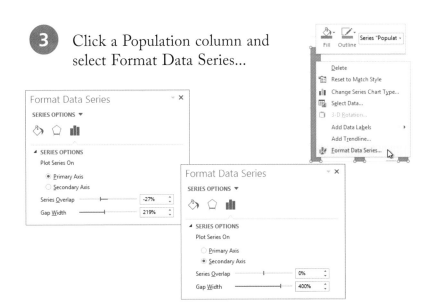

4 Choose Plot Series On Secondary Axis, and adjust Gap Width to 400%

5 Use the Chart Tools Format tab and Add Chart Element to edit, format and position the titles for the chart, the axes and the legend

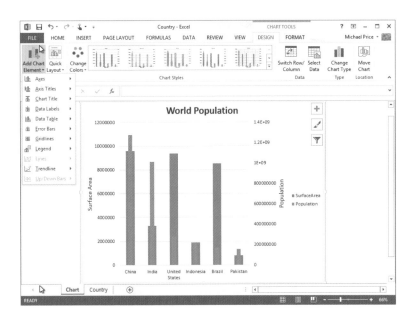

Import a List

The Country worksheet used as an example includes the Capital column, which provides a link to a list of cities. This list is available as a text file, so it can be imported.

The sample worksheet, shows the Capital as a City ID that references an external table of city names and other details.

1 Select a cell marking the start of an empty section of the worksheet, and then click the Data tab

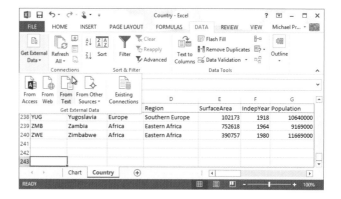

2 Click Get External Data and choose From Text

3 Locate the text file, click Import, then apply the Text Import Wizard (see page 88)

The text is transferred into the worksheet as a named range, using the name of the external text file, for example City.

4 Click OK to place the data in the current worksheet, at the location selected initially

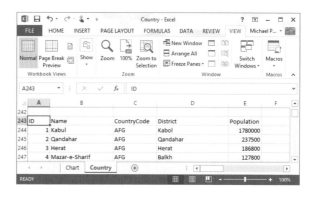

Create a Table

1 Click a cell within the data range and select the Insert tab, then click the Table button

Hot tip

To make it easier to manage and analyze the data in the list, you can turn the range of cells into an Excel table.

2 Click Yes to confirm the range and accept headers

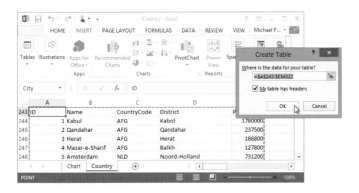

Don't forget

When you create a table from a data range, any connection with the external data source will be removed.

3 The table will be created (using the default style)

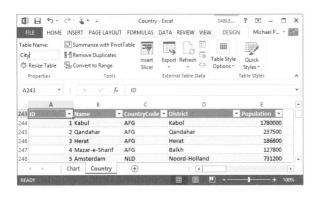

Hot tip

Change the default name (Table1 or similar) to something that's more relevant to the content, e.g. City.

Add Totals to Table

1 Click a cell within the country data and select Insert, Table, then rename the new table as Country

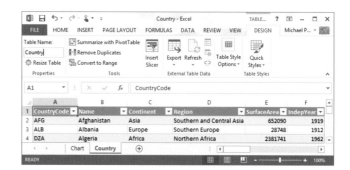

2 Select the Table Tools Design tab, then click the box for the Total Row, displayed at the end of the table

(101,	Average
(102,	Count numbers
(103,	Count
(104,	Max
(105,	Min
(107,	StdDev
(109,	Sum
(110,	Variance

3 Select the Total box for Name, click the arrow and choose the appropriate function, e.g. Count

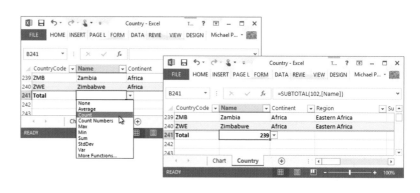

...cont'd

4 Select the Sum function for columns with numerical values, such as SurfaceArea, Population, or GNP

5 You can combine functions, such as Min and Max, to show the range of values in a column, e.g. IndepYear

6 When a column contains a set of discrete values, such as Continent or Region, you can calculate the number of unique values it contains

This is an array formula that counts the number of times each particular value in the column is repeated, and uses these repeats to build up a count of the number of distinct values in the column.

Hot tip

You do not use the column and row labels to specify cells and ranges, you use the header name for the column (enclosed in square brackets).

Don't forget

You can use any Excel function in the total boxes, not just the set of subfunctions in Subtotal.

Hot tip

You type an array formula without the enclosing curly braces { }, then press Ctrl + Shift + Enter, instead of the usual Enter, and the braces are added automatically.

Computed Column

You can insert a column in the table without affecting other ranges, data or tables in the worksheet.

If you select a cell in the last column of the table, you can insert a column to the left or the right.

1 Click in the Population column, select Home, click Insert, and choose Insert Table Columns to the Left

2 The new column is inserted and named Column1

The column names are used in the formulas, so it is best to choose meaningful names.

3 Select the new column header, type a new name, such as Density, and press Enter

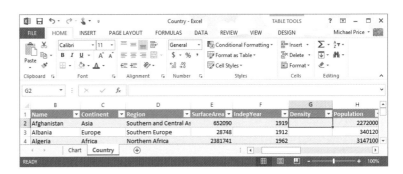

4 Click in the first cell of the column, and type =, then click the Population cell in the same row

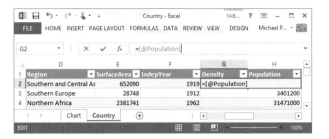

The cell that you select is referenced as the current row of Population, in the form: [@Population]. The next cell you select is referenced as: [@SurfaceArea].

5 Type /, then click the SurfaceArea cell in the row

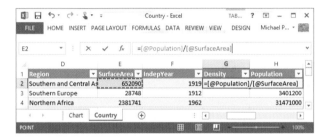

The result is the population density (people per square kilometer). You can format the values in the cells, for example as two decimal places.

G
Density ▼
34.84
118.31
13.21
341.71
166.67
10.33

6 Press Enter, the expression is evaluated and copied to all the other cells in the table column

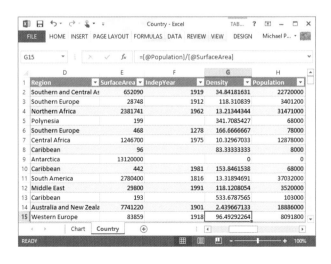

The formula in each cell refers to [@ColName], which is the current row for the named column.

103

Table Lookup

You can look up values in a table, and insert them in another table or data range.

The Country table contains a city code number for the capital city of each country, rather than the actual city name.

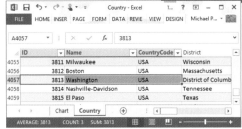

The names are stored in the City table, which has details of more than 4000 cities.

To display the name of the capital city alongside the city number, in the Country table:

1. Insert a table column next to the Capital column and change its name to CapitalCity

Click in the adjacent Code2 column and apply Insert Table Columns to the Left (see page 102).

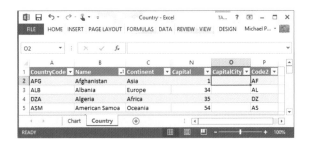

VLOOKUP is the vertical-lookup function, used when the values are stored in columns.

2. Click the first cell of the new column and type the expression =VLOOKUP(

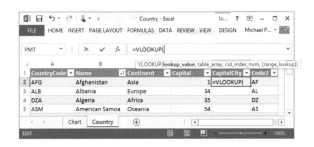

...cont'd

3 Click the adjacent cell in the Capital column, then type the expression ,City,2,0)

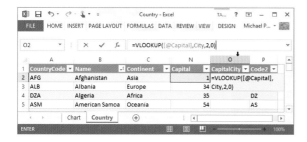

The table reference [@Capital] is the Capital number from the current row. The other parameters are City (the table name), 2 (the column with the actual name) and 0 (the code for Exact Match).

4 Press Enter, and the capital city name is added on all rows in the Country table, not just the current row

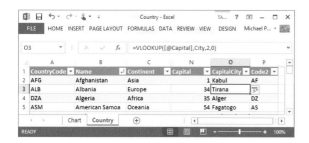

5 Scroll down to check the entries for particular countries, the United States (Washington) or the United Kingdom (London), for example

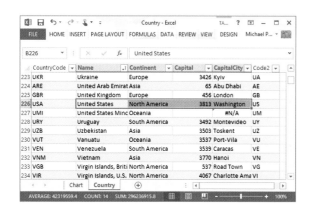

If the area does not have a capital city (e.g. United States Minor Outlying Islands) then the value #N/A is entered, to show no match found.

Manage Data Using Access

If you have large amounts of data, or complex functions to handle, you may need the more comprehensive Access 2013.

1 Select Access from the Start screen or the Taskbar, and you are greeted by a range of database templates

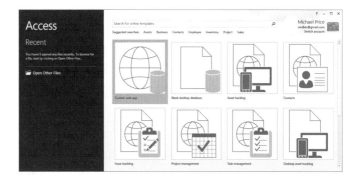

Hot tip

You'll find Access 2013 in the Professional editions of Office 2013. It appears as a tile on the Start screen, and you can also pin it to the Taskbar on the Desktop.

2 Select a category such as Assets to display a list of related templates available on the Internet

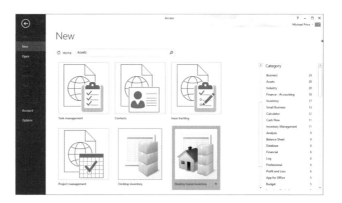

Hot tip

A default name such as Datebase1 will be assigned, but you can change this before you click the Create button.

3 Select a template to view details

4 When you've found the template that you want to use, click the Create button

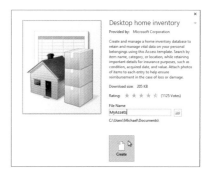

...cont'd

5 The selected template is downloaded to your computer

6 Access prepares the template for use as a new database

7 The database is opened with active content disabled

The template will be stored in the recent templates area and will be immediately available for reuse when you select File, New to create a database.

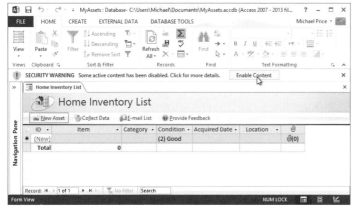

8 Click Enable Content to enable the VBA macros in the template and ready the database for updating

Do not enable content in databases that you download from Internet websites, unless you are sure that the source of the file is trustworthy.

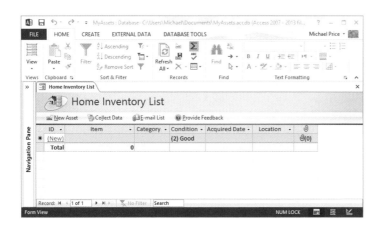

Add Records

You can type directly
into the cells of the
asset table if you wish,
rather than using
the form.

You can attach
links to associated
documents, or display
a photograph of the
asset, if you wish. Click
the Attachments box
and select Manage
Attachments.

1 Click New Asset to add
an entry to the Current
Assets database

2 Enter the details for the item, selecting from a list of
values on fields with an arrow, e.g. Category

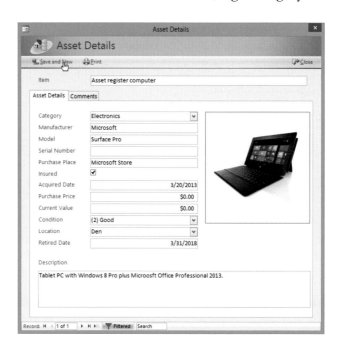

3 Click Save and New, to save the current record and
begin a new one, or click Close to return to the list

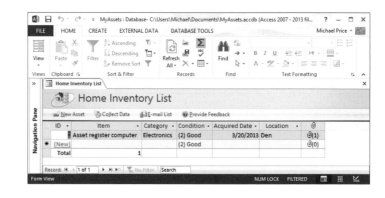

The current record is
automatically saved
when you click Close,
even if all the details
are not completed.

6 Presentations

Build a presentation, slide by slide, apply themes to create a consistent effect, and use animation to focus attention on particular points. Use a second monitor for a presenter view., and take advantage of templates. Print handouts, rehearse the show, to get timings, and create an automatic show.

Start a Presentation

To start PowerPoint and create a presentation:

1 Select the PowerPoint tile on the Start screen or the icon on the Taskbar

2 Select the Blank Presentation and Click to add title, then type the title for your slide show, e.g. Origami

Hot tip

When PowerPoint opens, it presents a single blank title slide, ready for you to begin a new presentation.

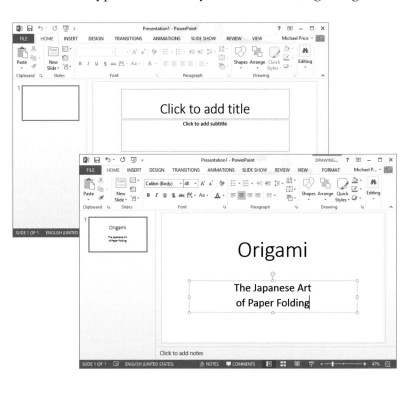

Don't forget

By default, the presentation starts with a title slide, where two text boxes are predefined. If you don't want a particular text box, just ignore it – it won't appear on the slide unless you edit the text.

3 Click to add subtitle, and type the subtitle for your slide show, e.g. The Japanese Art of Paper Folding

4 Select the Home tab and click the New Slide button in the Slides group

5 A new slide, with text boxes for title and content, will be added to the slide show

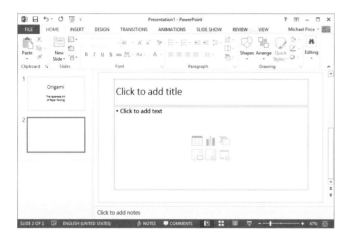

The new slide has option buttons to insert a table, chart, SmartArt graphic, or picture from a file, clip art or media clip. See page 113 for an example.

Hot tip

6 Click on the prompts and add the title The History of Origami, then type bullet points to give details

111

Press Enter to add a new bullet item, and then press the Tab key to move to the next lower level of bullet items

Click within a bullet item and press Shift + Tab to move it up (promote it) to the next higher level.

Don't forget

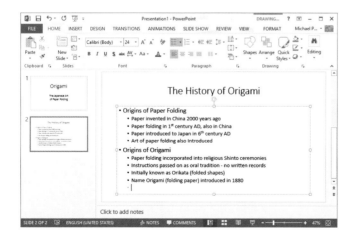

Expand the Slide

1 Click the button to Save your presentation

2 Continue to add items, you'll see the text size and spacing adjusted to fit the text onto the slide

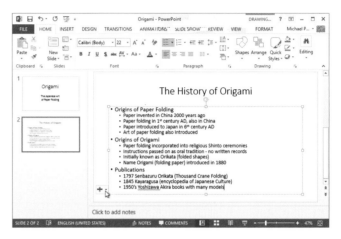

Alternatively, you can choose to stop fitting text to the placeholder, to continue on a new slide, or to change to a two-column format.

3 When the slide fills, click the AutoFit Options button and click Split Text Between Two Slides

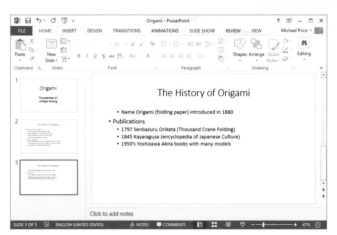

The text size and spacing will be re-adjusted to take advantage of the extra space available.

4 A new slide is inserted, with the same layout and title as the first slide, with bullet items split across

Insert a Picture

1 Select Home then click the arrow on the New Slide button in the Slides group to display the options

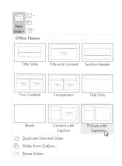

2 Choose a slide layout, such as Picture with Caption

Click the icon to add the picture

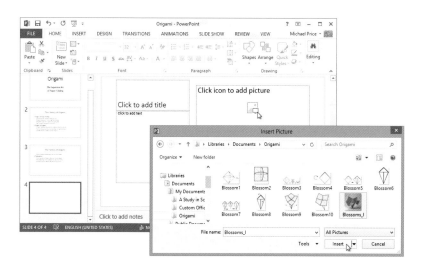

Locate and select the image file and click Insert, then select Click to add title, and Click to add text

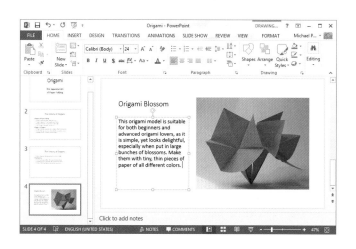

Hot tip

There are nine standard layouts for slides, so you can select the one that's most appropriate for the specific content planned for each slide.

Don't forget

The title and the text you add provide the caption for the inserted image.

Don't forget

Insert the other slides needed to complete your presentation.

Apply a Theme

By default, slides have a plain background, but you can choose a more effective theme and apply it to all your slides.

The selected theme is temporarily applied to the current slide, to help you choose the most effective theme.

1 Select the Design tab, and move the mouse pointer over each of the themes, to see the effect

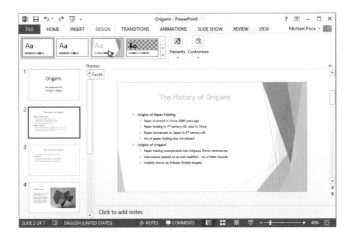

2 You can scroll the list to display additional themes, change the colors, fonts, and effects for the current theme, and modify the type of background style used

You can right-click your selected theme and choose to apply it to selected slides, or set the theme as the default for your future slides.

Apply to All Slides
Apply to Selected Slides
Delete...
Set as Default Theme
Add Gallery to Quick Access Toolbar

3 Click the preferred theme to apply it to all of the slides in the presentation

...cont'd

To select the transition effects between slides:

1 Select the Transitions tab and review the options – starting with None, Cut, Fade, Push

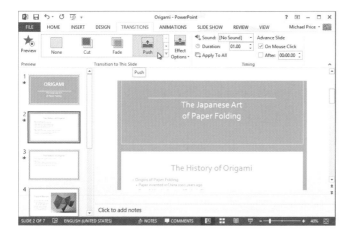

Hot tip

Move the mouse pointer over an effect to see it demonstrated on the current slide, for example Push from bottom.

Click the up and down arrows to view another of the 12 rows of effects

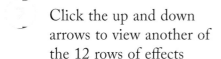

3 Click an effect to assign it to the current slide

By default, you advance to the next slide when you press the mouse key, but you can adjust this for individual slides.

4 Clear the On Mouse Click box to disable the mouse-key for the current slide

5 Select to Advance Slide After the specified time

Click the Apply To All button to apply the settings to all the slides in the presentation

Whatever the setting, you can always advance the slide show by pressing one of the keyboard shortcuts, such as N (next), Enter, Page Down, right arrow, or spacebar.

Don't forget

When you select a transition, the Effects Options button is enabled, so you can choose variations of that transition.

Effect Options ▾

Don't forget

If you have specified animation effects for individual elements on a slide (see page 116), the Advance function invokes the next animation, rather than the next slide.

Animations

You can apply animation effects to individual parts of a slide.

1 Select the Animations tab, pick a slide with bullet items. Note the Animate button is grayed (inactive)

The animation can be at Entrance, for Emphasis, or at Exit, and may be applied All At Once or By 1st Level Paragraph.

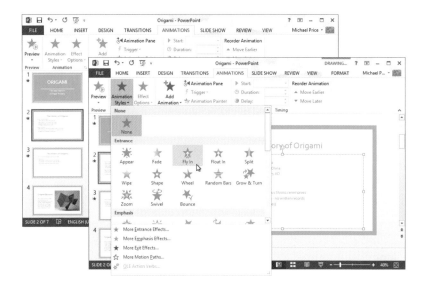

If you apply animation within the slide, you may want to enable automatic advance, unless you plan to manually display each line of the slide.

2 Select the text box with the bullet items, and the Animate button is activated

3 Click the down arrow on the Animate box and choose, for example, Fly In, By 1st Level Paragraph, then click the Preview button to observe the effect

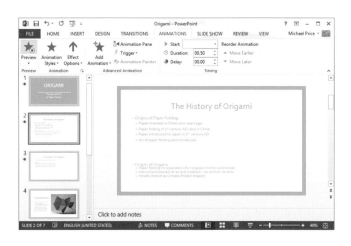

Select Add Animation in the Advanced Animation group, if you want to apply additional effects to the slide.

Run the Show

When you've added all the slides you need, you can try running the complete show, to see the overall effect.

1 Select the Slide Show tab and click the From the Beginning button in the Start Slide Show group

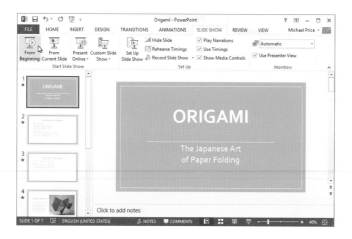

The slides are displayed full-screen, with the transition and animation effects that you selected

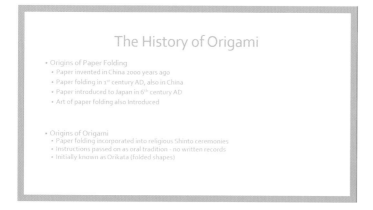

Click the mouse or keyboard shortcut to advance the slide show, animation by animation, or wait the delay time

4 Review each slide in turn to the end of the show

You can also press F5 to run the slide show from the beginning, press Shift + F5 to run from the current slide, or press Esc to terminate.

You'll see the selected transition effect between the slides, in this example the effect is Dissolve.

When the slide show finishes, a black screen is presented, with the message: End of slide show, click to exit.

End of slide show, click to exit.

Other Views

Hot tip

This view is very helpful when you have a larger number of slides, since you can simply drag slides into their new positions.

Don't forget

Each slide and its notes will be displayed on a single sheet, which can be printed to make a very useful handout.

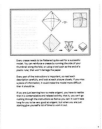

Hot tip

There's also a Reading View button, provided in the Presentation Views group on the Views tab, which allows you to view the slide show.

1 Select the View tab and select Slide Sorter to display all the slides, so you can rearrange their sequence

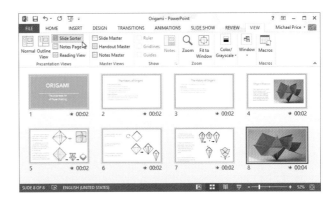

2 Select the Notes Page view to see the current slide with its notes and prompts for presenter

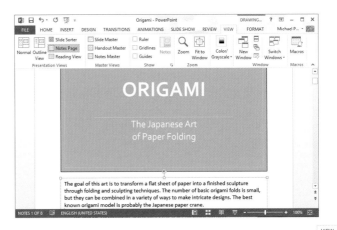

3 Click the Zoom button and select a zoom level then click OK (or drag the slider on the zoom bar), to examine the slide or notes in detail

4 Select Fit and click OK (or click the Fit to Window button) to resize and show the whole page

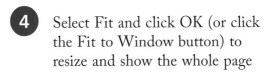

5 To switch back to the view with slide bar and current slide, click the Normal button

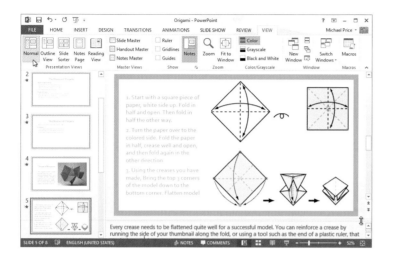

The view you select will be retained when you select another tab, so you should revert to the required view before leaving.

6 To reveal more of the notes area, click and drag the separator bar upwards

Click the Outline tab to see the text content of the slides, giving a summary view of the presentation

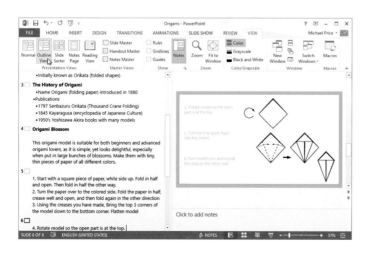

The buttons to the left of the Zoom bar are another way to select Normal, Slide Sorter, Reading, and Slide Show views.

Scroll the summary area as needed to view all slides

Presenter View

1 Select the Slide Show tab, and click the box to enable the Use Presenter View option

If your system has dual-monitor support, you can run your presentation from one monitor, while your audience views it on a second monitor (or on a projector screen).

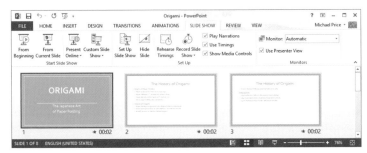

2 If you have attached a second monitor, right-click the desktop and select Screen Resolution

3 Click the Multiple Displays box and select Extend these displays

When you change your display settings, you must confirm to keep the changes within 15 seconds or the changes will be reversed.

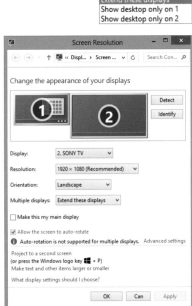

4 Click Apply, then OK and click Keep Changes when prompted

5 Select Slide Show and click From Beginning to run the slide show on two monitors

The first monitor gives the presenter's view, with the current slide and its associated notes, plus a preview of the next slide. There's also a Slide bar, to change the slide sequences.

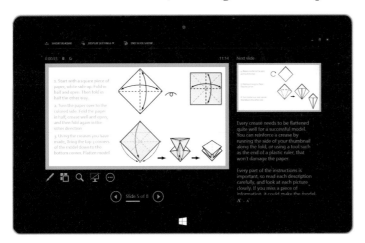

The second monitor is for your audience and displays the current slides in full-screen mode.

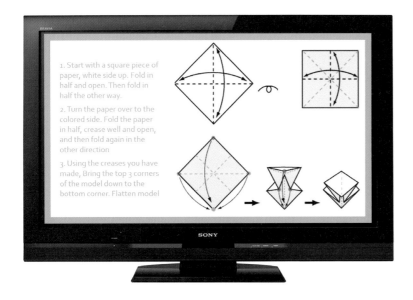

Don't forget

If you do not have a second monitor or projector attached you can still select Presenter View and press Alt + F5 to run the show from the presenter's view only.

Hot tip

Use the Zoom button to enlarge the notes and make them easier to read while giving the presentation.

Choose a Template

Hot tip

Templates provide pre-built presentations, which can be adapted to your needs. They also offer examples of useful PowerPoint techniques.

1 Select the File tab, then click New, to display the templates provided

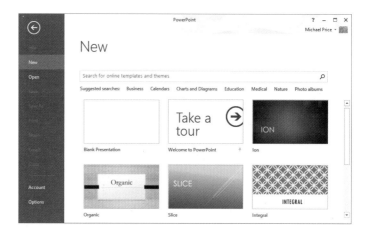

2 Select a template, for example Slice, to see details and view images using the themes and colors offered

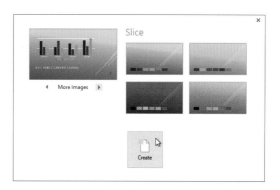

Don't forget

You can also enter your own keywords if you want to make a more specific search for suitable templates.

3 To make a presentation using the template, click Create, otherwise close to review other templates

4 You can use the suggested categories, for example Business, to search for online templates and themes

...cont'd

5 PowerPoint searches online for relevant templates and themes

6 Thumbnails and links are displayed for the items located, and the associated subcategories are listed

PowerPoint shows the number of templates in each subcategory, and you can select these to identify more closely a suitable template.

Select, for example, the Business plan presentation, and you'll see twelve slides on various topics

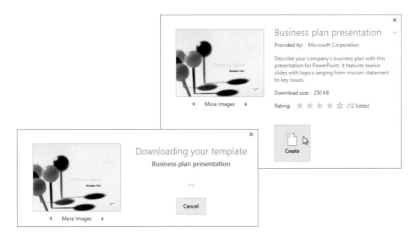

The Templates that you download and review will be added to the templates displayed when you select File, New in future sessions.

Click Create and the template will be downloaded and a presentation based on it will be opened

Use the Template

Don't forget

You can revise the text, add and replace images with your own pictures, and make your own presentation based on the chosen template.

1 When you create a new presentation with a template, it opens showing the predefined slides and content

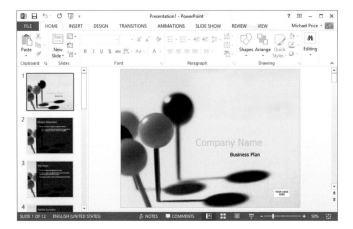

2 You can edit any of the slides, remove unnecessary slides or add new slides (using the theme if desired)

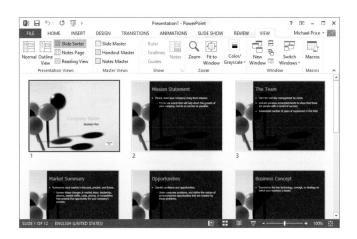

Don't forget

The template will be retained in its original form in case you want to use it again in the future.

3 To resequence the slides, select View and then click Slide Sorter

4 Save under a new name to preserve the changes

Print the Slide Show

Select the File tab, then click the Print button to specify the printer and other printing options

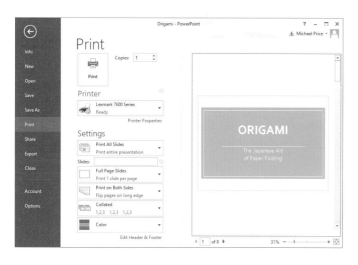

Hot tip

Print Preview is provided, and you can use the scroll bar to view the slides in your presentation. The Zoom bar allows you to take a closer view.

Select the printer you want to use, or take the default

Enter slide numbers or ranges, and the Print All Slides setting changes to Custom Range

Click the Print Layout button to choose what type of document to print

You can print full page slides, slides with notes, or an outline

If you select Handouts, specify the number of slides to a page, and the order (horizontal or vertical)

You can also select Frames Slides, Scale to Fit Paper, and High Quality printing

Don't forget

You can choose to print the document in grayscale, or pure black-and-white, even if the presentation itself is in full color.

Rehearse Timings

To establish the timings for each slide, you need to rehearse the presentation and record the times for each step.

1 Select the Slide Show tab and click Rehearse Timings, which is in the Set Up group

2 The slide show runs full-screen in manual mode, with the timer superimposed in the top left corner

3 Advance each slide or animation, allowing for viewing and narration, etc., and times are recorded

4 When the presentation finishes, you can choose to keep the slide timings for subsequent viewings

5 The Slide Sorter displays, with Advance Slides After selected, and the individual timing for each slide

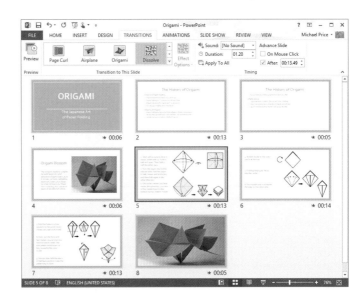

Hot tip

You can make the presentation easier to run by assigning timings to the slides, so that it can run automatically.

Don't forget

The timer shows the duration so far for the individual slide, and for the presentation as a whole.

126

Hot tip

Select the Transitions tab to make further adjustments to the times for particular slides.

Save As Options

1 Select the File tab and the Info view is selected, with all the details of the presentation file

2 Click Save As, and then click the box labeled Save as type, to see what file formats are supported

3 The PowerPoint Presentation (.pptx) format is the default, and is the file type that is designed for presentation editing

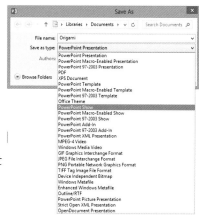

4 Select the PowerPoint Show (.ppsx) format for the file type that is protected from modification. This will open in the Slide Show view

There are several forms you can save your PowerPoint 2013 Presentation in, including ways to share it with other users.

Save in the PowerPoint 97–2003 Show format (or Presentation format), to allow users with older versions of PowerPoint to view (or modify) the presentation.

Package for CD

1 With the required presentation open, select the File tab, Save & Send, then Package Presentation for CD

Hot tip

You can also create a PDF or XMS document or create a video of the presentation, to send as email attachments perhaps, or create printed handouts.

2 Type a name for the CD, add more presentations, if required, then click Copy to Folder

3 Edit the folder name and location, if necessary, then click OK

4 The presentation files are added to the folder, along with all the files needed to run the PowerPoint Viewer

Don't forget

The package will include any linked or embedded items required, such as videos, sound recordings and fonts.

5 Confirm that you have everything you need, then go back to Package for CD (see step 2) and this time select Copy to CD. You'll be prompted to insert a blank CD

7 Office Extras

OneNote is your interactive notebook. Other extras include the Office Tools for managing and maintaining your copy of Office, with other tools provided as apps from Windows Store.

OneNote 2003 was stand-alone. OneNote 2007 was in three of the Office 2007 editions. OneNote 2010 was in all Office 2010 editions except Starter. OneNote 2013 is in all editions of Office 2013 including Office RT, Office 365 and the online Office Web Apps.

OneNote 2013

A later addition to the Office applications, OneNote is now fully incorporated into all the Office 2013 editions.

The digital version of a pocket notebook, OneNote gives you the means to capture, organize, and access all of the information you need for a specific task or project, personal or collaborative, and in whatever the format of the data – typed, written, audio, video, figures or photographs.

To start using OneNote 2013 on your computer:

1 Select the OneNote tile from the Start screen, or click the OneNote icon on the Taskbar

2 OneNote starts up and opens your initial notebook called My Notebook, with the Quick Notes section selected and the general advice page OneNote: one place for all your notes

This covers the following four topics:

- Take notes anywhere on the page
- Get organized and add sections and pages
- For more tips, review the 30-second videos
- Create your first page in the Quick Notes section and use it for random notes

OneNote offers four 30-second videos on these useful topics:
– Clip from the Web
– Plan a trip with others
– Search notes instantly
– Write notes on slides

...cont'd

3 Select the second advice page OneNote Basics

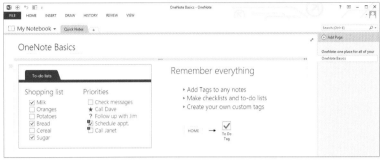

This covers additional topics including:

- Remember everything
- Collaborate with others
- Organize with tables
- Integrate with Outlook
- Add Excel spreadsheets
- Brainstorm without clutter

When you display this page the icon for the Send to OneNote tool is added onto the Taskbar

Click in the Start with OneNote box if you want this tool to always load when you launch OneNote

Hot tip

The first time it starts, OneNote copies folder OneNote Notebooks (containing your Personal notebook) to your Documents Library.

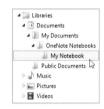

Hot tip

If the Send to OneNote is not displayed, select View and then click the button for Send to OneNote Tool in the Windows group.

Create a Notebook

You can create a new OneNote notebook from scratch:

1 Open OneNote, select the File tab, then click New

Hot tip

The default location for Computer is the OneNote Notebooks subfolder, in the Documents folder for the active user name.

2 Choose where to put the notebook (SkyDrive, Computer or Add a Place) and provide the name, e.g. Planning

3 Confirm the location then click Create Notebook

Don't forget

OneNote doesn't provide any content for you or offer any templates by default, though you can locate OneNote templates at the Office website.

The notebook opens with a new section and an untitled page, ready to add notes, new pages, and new sections, or to send documents or clips from other applications.

...cont'd

As with most Office applications, you will find it easier and more instructive to start from a suitable template.

1 Select the Help icon on the Title bar at the right (or press F1)

2 Select More in the Getting started section

3 Internet Explorer opens **office.microsoft.com** at the page Get started with OneNote 2013

4 Select Templates to show all Office templates

5 Select More, OneNote to display related templates

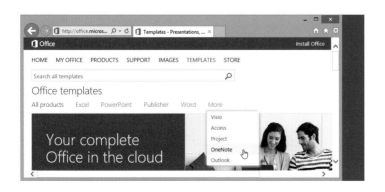

Hot tip

With OneNote, you need to visit the **Office.com** or other websites to find templates. They are not shown when you select File, New to create a notebook.

Don't forget

The Template command shows templates for all the Office applications, so you need to select the specific application to restrict the list to relevant templates only.

Download a Template

1 The Office website offers many OneNote templates

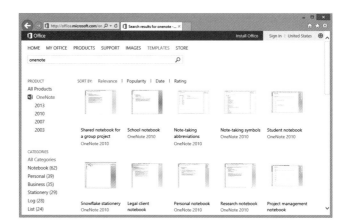

There are templates for all versions of OneNote, and these can all be used with OneNote 2013.

You may get a message saying that a Pop-up has been blocked. Click the message and select to allow pop-ups. If you are not sure of the site, choose Allow once.

Internet Explorer blocked a pop-up from office.microsoft.com.

Options for this site ▼   ✕
Allow once
Always allow
More settings

2 Select a suitable template to view its details, then click Download to add it

Home improvement journal
OneNote 2010

3 Amend name or location if desired and click Save

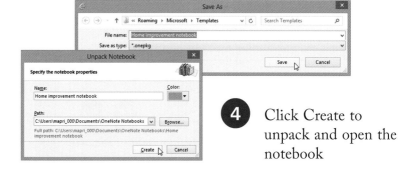

4 Click Create to unpack and open the notebook

...cont'd

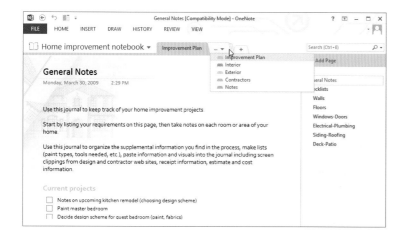

Don't forget

The section names are shown on the tabs. You may need to click the down arrow on the tab bar to display some of the sections.

The template is based on an older version of OneNote so opens in compatibility mode. To change the format of the new notebook:

1 Right-click the Notebook tab and select Properties

Hot tip

If you are sharing the notebook with users of an older OneNote, do not convert the format.

2 Click Convert to 2010-2013 and the file will be converted to the latest format and saved

Don't forget

Once you've opened or created a notebook, it is reopened when OneNote starts, unless you select File, Info, right-click Settings for that notebook, and select Close.

OneNote App

You can read and create notebooks on your Windows 8 computer, even if it doesn't have a copy of Microsoft Office, if you install the Windows 8 OneNote app.

1 Visit the Windows Store from the Start screen, search for OneNote, then select Productivity category

2 Select the free OneNote app to review the details

3 Select the Install button to download the app and install it on your system

4 A tile is added to the Start screen

Don't forget

There's a Windows 8 app that allows access to notebooks on the SkyDrive. This makes it easy to share notebooks with computers that do not have a copy of Microsoft Office installed.

Hot tip

This OneNote app can be installed on Windows RT computers as well as Windows 8 computers. There are equivalent apps available for mobile devices such as the Windows Phones.

5 Select the new OneNote tile and the Windows 8 app opens an initial notebook with helpful advice

There's no Ribbon in the OneNote app but you can touch or click the button to display the Radial Menu which is particularly designed for touch interactions.

6 Select the video link to view an introduction which emphasizes that it keeps everything on the SkyDrive

7 Right-click or swipe up on the OneNote screen and select Notebooks from the Apps bar to list any other notebooks that may be stored on your SkyDrive

You can also access the notebooks in your SkyDrive using the Web App version of OneNote (see page 230).

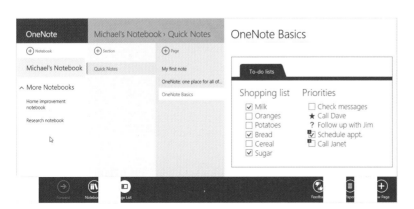

Office Tools

Hot tip

The Office suite includes a set of tools, as well as applications. You can check which tools have been installed on your system.

New

Don't forget

The tools available vary by edition. These are the tools in Office 2013 Professional Plus. Other editions may have fewer tools. The Office 2013 student edition in Windows RT, for example, has just two (Language Preferences and Upload Center).

To see which Office tools are installed on your system:

1 Right-click the Start screen and select All apps from the Apps bar

2 Right-click an Office 2013 tool such as the Upload Center and select Open file location on the Apps bar

3 You find shortcuts for the Office tools, in the folder C:\ProgramData\Microsoft\Windows\Start Menu\ Programs\Microsoft Office 2013\Office 2013 Tools\

You can check to see what other tools may be included with your edition of Office 2013.

1 From the Desktop, display the Charms bar, select Settings, then select Control Panel

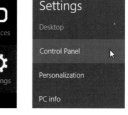

2 Locate the Programs category and click Uninstall a program. There are also options to Add, Change or Repair programs

...cont'd

Select the Microsoft Office entry and click Change

4 Select Add or Remove Features and click Continue

Scroll the installation options and review the entries for Office Shared Features and the Office Tools

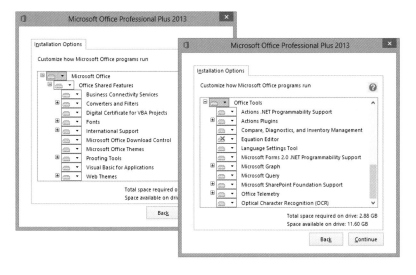

When you've finished the review, click [X] to Close

Hot tip

You can use Uninstall a program to explore the Office 2013 configuration options for all editions of Office 2013 except Office 2013 RT, which is installed as part of the Windows RT operating system.

Don't forget

If any of the Shared Features or Tools are shown as not installed, you can select Run from my computer and allow Configuration to complete the installation.

Otherwise, Close and Cancel Configuration.

Language Preferences

Office supports multiple languages, for editing, for display, for help, and for screen tips.

You can also set Office language preferences, by selecting File, Options, Language, from within any Office application.

1 This document includes text in French, seen as errors by the default English (US) spelling checker

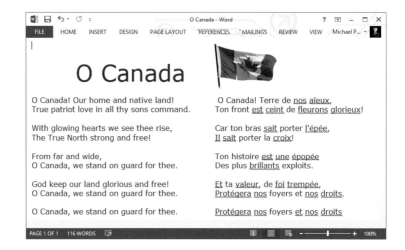

You have similar problems when you work with documents that have text in other languages, or when you use a system with a different language installed, e.g. when traveling.

To check the languages enabled, and to add a new language:

1 From the Start screen, display the All apps screen and select Office Language Preferences

2 Click Add Languages and choose the language

...cont'd

Click the Add button, then select and add any other languages you require

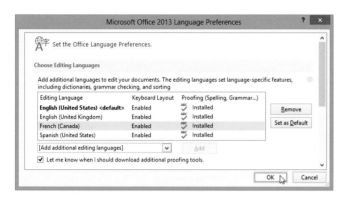

Don't forget

You may be required to enable a keyboard layout appropriate for the language added.

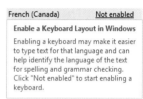

Click OK, then OK again to apply the changes, then close and restart any open Office applications

5 Any text in the new languages will be detected, and the appropriate spell checker will be employed

Hot tip

If required, you can select any portions of the text not properly detected, then click Review, Language, Set Proofing Language, and make the appropriate choice.

Spreadsheet Compare can determine, for example, when rows or columns have been inserted or deleted and report this rather than highlighting consequential differences in cell contents.

You might choose two versions of the same spreadsheet to identify amendments that may have been made, or two spreadsheets with similar contents, in this case country populations in 2000 and 2013.

Compare Spreadsheets

The Spreadsheet Compare tool lets you pick any two workbooks and compare them very quickly. The differences between spreadsheets are categorized so you can focus on important changes, such as changes to formulas.

To see the tool in action:

1 Select Spreadsheet Compare from the All apps screen

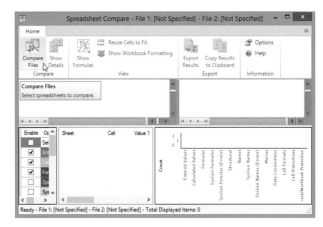

2 Click the button to Compare Files

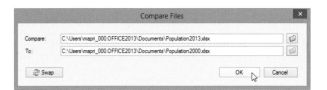

3 Select the Browse buttons in turn to locate the two spreadsheets that you'd like to compare

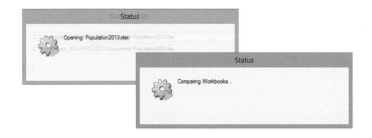

4 The two workbooks are opened and compared, and the results are displayed side-by-side

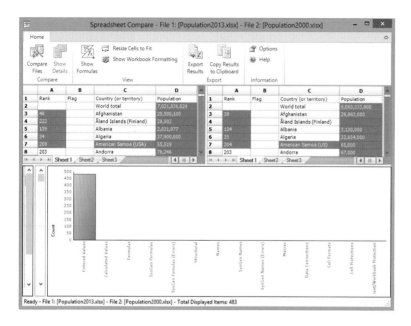

Hot tip

In this example it's only data values (populations, ranks and some country names) that are flagged as different.

Hot tip

You can choose to display the formulas in each cell rather than the values, to help identify possible causes for changes.

5 Spreadsheet Compare can identify complex changes

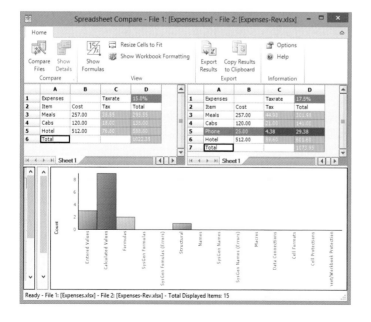

Show Formulas

Don't forget

Here the tax rate has changed, and an extra line has been entered. The tool understands that some items get displaced, and only flags the actual differences, e.g. in the tax and the totals.

Database Compare

This tool provides facilities for comparing the structures of different versions of an Access database.

Hot tip

You may need to install some developments tools such as Microsoft. NET Framework and Microsoft Report Viewer before you can run the Database Compare tool.

1 Select the Database Compare tool from the All apps screen

2 Specify the Access databases that you wish to compare, and choose which elements to review

3 Click Compare, to generate a database comparison report

Don't forget

The reports concentrate on changes to the design of the tables, queries and other components, rather than changes to the data content of the tables. This allows you to identify changes made by others if the support of the database is shared.

Other Tools

The following tools may also be included in your Office:

Office Upload Center

This allows you to check the status of files that get uploaded to web servers (your SkyDrive for example). Microsoft Office first saves such files locally in the Office Document Cache before it starts the upload, which means that you can save changes and continue working even if offline or on a slow network connection. The Office Upload Center keeps track of progress and actions needed.

Hot tip

The Document Cache and the Upload Center are very useful when you are traveling and do not always have access to the Internet.

Telemetry Dashboard and Telemetry Log

Office Telemetry is a new compatibility monitoring framework. When an Office document or solution is loaded, used, closed, or raises an error in Office 2013 applications, the application adds a record about the event to the Telemetry Log associated with each user. Inventory and usage data is also tracked. The Telemetry Dashboard amalgamates the information for all the users so that the technical administrator can assess the compatibility of the whole system.

Office Telemetry is a sophisticated system that is based on Excel 2013 workbooks but also requires access to an SQL Server.

Lync Recording Manager

This is used with the Lync 2013 application (see page 222) to manage the recordings of online meetings and conferences conducted using the instant messaging and communications facilities that are built into Lync. It is for the business environment and requires Microsoft Exchange Server for full function.

These are just some of the products that Microsoft has made available for a time as Office Tools, and then decided to remove or replace.

With Windows 8, the emphasis is on apps provided through the Windows Store, so the facilities provided via the Office Tools can be expected to reduce further with future versions.

Tools Removed from Office

A number of tools have been removed, with some being replaced by alternative features in the Office applications, or by tools and utilities available elsewhere. For example:

Microsoft Binder
This was designed as a container system for storing related documents in a single file, but was discontinued after Office XP. OneNote offers more comprehensive, functions.

Microsoft Office Document Image Writer
This was a virtual printer for Microsoft Office and other documents, to store them in TIFF or Microsoft Document Imaging Format. It was discontinued with Office 2010.

Microsoft Office Document Imaging
This allowed you to edit scanned documents. It was discontinued with Office 2010.

Microsoft Office Document Scanning
This scanning and OCR (Optical Character Recognition) application was discontinued with Office 2010. However, OCR facilities are included in OneNote.

Microsoft Office Picture Manager
This provided photo management and enhancement software but with Office 2013 it has been removed and replaced by the various Photos apps available from the Windows Store and by Windows Live Photo Gallery. This product is part of the Windows Essentials (see **http://windows.microsoft. com/en-us/windows-live/essentials**) which are available for Windows 8 but not Windows RT systems.

Clip Organizer
This was used to collect and store clip art, photos, animations, videos, and other media to use in documents, presentations, spreadsheets and other files. It has been effectively replaced by the Office 2013 Insert functions.

8 Email

The first time you use Outlook, you specify your email account. Then you can receive messages, save attachments, print messages, issue replies, and update your address book, while protecting yourself from spam messages that might be targeted at your account. You can add a standard signature note to your messages. You can also subscribe to RSS feeds.

Starting Outlook

The Microsoft Outlook program provides the email and time management functions in Office 2013. To start the application:

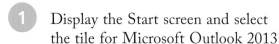

1 Display the Start screen and select the tile for Microsoft Outlook 2013

To make this application quicker and easier to find, add it as a shortcut on the Taskbar.

1 Locate the Outlook entry on the Start screen, as described above, then right-click and select the Pin to Taskbar button

2 The associated icon will be added to the Taskbar, beside any other applications you may have selected

To start Microsoft Outlook from the Taskbar:

1 Display the Desktop, click the Microsoft Outlook icon on the Taskbar and the application will launch

Don't forget

Outlook 2013 is found in all editions of Office 2013 except the Home and Student edition (including the edition supplied with Windows RT 8.0). Systems with that edition would use the Mail app to send and receive email.

Hot tip

If you have Office 2013 Professional Plus or an Office 365 business edition, the Lync instant messaging application will also start up when you start Outlook.

...cont'd

The first time you start Outlook, it helps you to define the email accounts you want to manage using this application.

Hot tip

Outlook detects when no accounts are defined, and runs the Startup wizard to obtain details of your email account.

1 Click Next to start, select Yes to set up Outlook to connect an email account, then click Next again

2 Type your name, your email address, and your password and click Next to set up your account

Don't forget

You could manually configure your account, but the easiest way to add the account is to let the wizard establish the settings for you.

Configure Server Settings

Your email account may use POP3 connections, where messages are fully downloaded to your computer, or IMAP, where messages are listed on your computer but not downloaded until you open them.

For some email accounts, those from **Yahoo.com** for example, the wizard may be unable to detect the settings. You will need to select the option to Change account settings and enter the information provided by your email supplier.

Outlook is completing the setup for your account.
✓ Establishing network connection
✓ Searching for maprice@yahoo.com settings
✗ Log on to server and send a test e-mail message
We are having trouble connecting to your account.
☑ Change account settings

1 The wizard identifies your Internet connection, and establishes the network connection

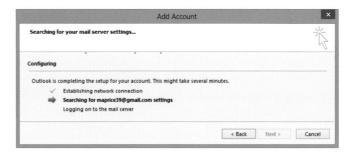

2 The wizard then searches for the server settings that support your email account

3 Finally, the wizard logs on to the server, using your account name and password, and sends a test message. Click Finish to ready your email account

Your First Messages

Outlook opens with the Inbox, showing your first messages, e.g. welcome and test messages from the ISP and Outlook.

Quick Access Toolbar   Tab bar   Title bar   Help   Ribbon

To-Do bar

Calendar

Appointment list

Task list

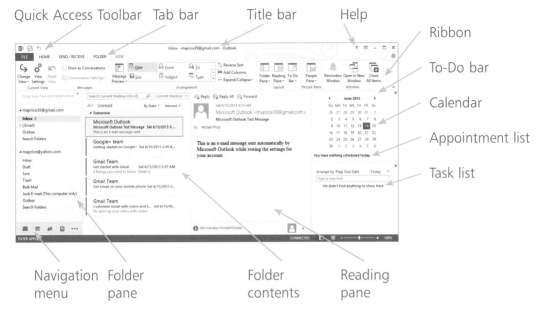

Navigation   Folder   Folder   Reading
menu   pane   contents   pane

Collapse the Folder pane and hide the To-Do bar, to provide more space to display more message content, or to cope with a smaller screen size. You may position the Reading Pane below the message list, or hide it altogether (see page 152).

Hot tip

Outlook may prevent automatic download of some pictures in the message. If you trust the source, you can choose to download the pictures.

Turn Off Reading Pane

1 Select View, Reading Pane, and choose Off, rather than Right or Bottom

2 Messages are left unread until opened

It is possible that the very act of reading an email message could release harmful software into your system. Turn off the Reading pane and review the message source and title before it is actually read, to avoid potential problems with spam and phishing emails (see pages 160-161).

3 Double-click (or select and press Enter) to open a message and display its contents

The messages that have been opened are listed with regular rather than bold and colored font.

4 Click the Close button at the top right

5 Click the Up or Down arrows on the Quick Access toolbar to switch to the previous or the next message

6 Alternatively, select File and then select Close from the action list in the back stage view

Request a Newsletter

You'll share your email address with friends, contacts, and organizations, to begin exchanging messages. You can also use your email address to request newsletters. For example:

1 Visit the website **http://thrillerwriters.org/** and select ITW, The Big Thrill to see newsletter details

2 Scroll down to the form to apply for a subscription

3 Enter your email address, first name and last name, and choose the format

4 Click the Subscribe button

5 An invitation is sent to your email

Hot tip

ITW is an honorary society of authors who write books, fiction and non fiction, broadly classified as thrillers. The website features a regular newsletter.

Don't forget

There may be a fee for the service in some cases, though, most often, the newsletters are provided free of charge, as in this example.

…cont'd

6 Double-click the email confirmation request message when it arrives in your Inbox

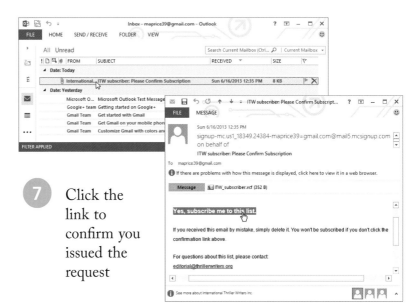

Don't forget

Your address could be provided, accidentally or deliberately, without your permission, so you must explicitly confirm you wish to subscribe.

7 Click the link to confirm you issued the request

8 The website is updated to confirm the subscription

9 A further email will arrive in your Inbox, completing the subscription

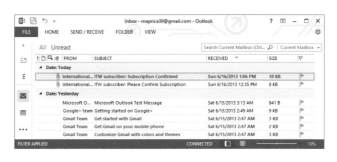

Hot tip

Retain this email, since it provides the links needed to change your details, or to unsubscribe, if you no longer wish to receive the newsletter.

Receive a Message

To check for any mail that may be waiting:

1 Open Outlook, select the Send/Receive tab, and click the Send/Receive button

2 New mail is downloaded and displayed in the Inbox

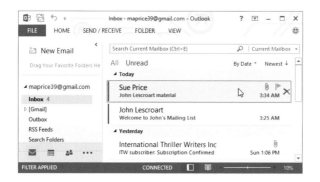

3 Double-click the message title to display contents

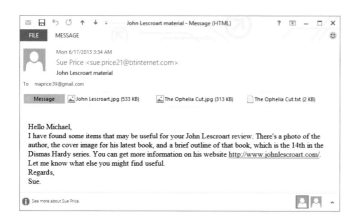

4 Right-click one of the attachments, and then select Save As to save that attachment

5 Specify the target folder (see page 156) and choose Save

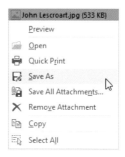

Don't forget

Depending on the settings, Outlook may automatically issue a Send/Receive when it starts up, and at intervals thereafter. You can also manually check for messages at any time.

Hot tip

Select the Send/Receive tab to get extra functions that give more control over the Send/Receive process.

Save All Attachments

To save all the attachments at once:

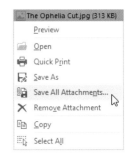

1 Open the message, right-click any attachment, and select Save All Attachments...

2 The list is displayed, with all the attachments selected

3 Press Ctrl, and click any of the attachments to adjust the selection if desired, then click OK to download the files

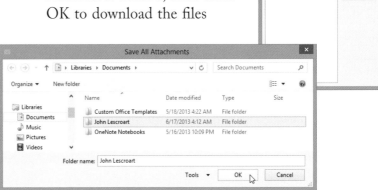

4 Locate the folder for the downloads (or click New Folder to insert a new folder), then click OK to save

5 Open the target folder in File Explorer to view the files that you have just saved

Print the Message

1 From the message, select File, then click Print

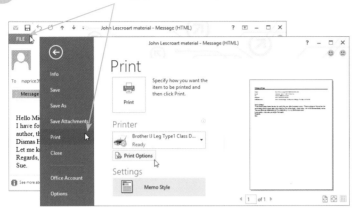

The File Print Preview shows how the message will appear on the page. Select Quick Print to send the message to the printer, using all the default settings.

Print

2 Click Print Options to change the printer or adjust print settings, e.g. number of copies

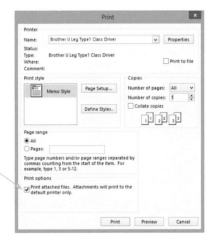

3 When you click to select the Print options box, you can also print the file attachments (on the default printer only)

4 For picture attachments, you can choose the print size of the image

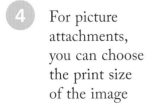

Each attachment will print as a separate print job, destined for the default printer. You can change the print size on each job, but you cannot combine the prints onto the same sheet.

Reply to the Message

You can click Reply to All. If you want to share the message with another person, click Forward.

The Compose mode of the Message Editor has additional tabs – Insert, Options, Format Text, and Review.

The message is moved to the Outbox, and when it has been sent, a copy goes to Sent Items. A Sent note is attached to the original message, the message icon is updated, and Outlook can keep track of the conversation.

1 When you want to reply to a message that you've opened, click the Reply button, in the Respond group on the Message tab

2 The message form opens with the email address and subject entered, and the cursor in the message area, to type your comments above the original text

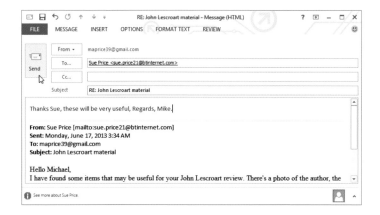

3 Complete your response and then click the Send button to transfer the response initially to the Outbox and then to the Sent folder upon completion

Note that the Reading Pane may be active in the Sent folder, even if it has been switched off in the Inbox, since the Reading Pane must be separately configured for each folder.

Add Address to Contacts

Whenever you receive an email, you can add the sender (and any other addressees) to your Outlook Contacts list.

1 Right-click the email address and select Add to Outlook Contacts

2 Review the data pre-entered, and add any extra information that you may have

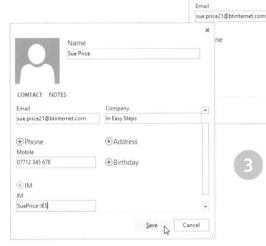

3 Click Save to record the details in the Outlook Contacts list

4 Open the Contacts folder to create or update entries

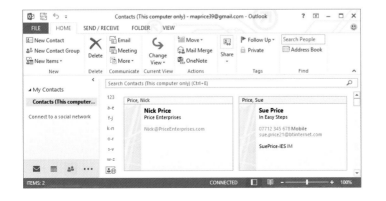

You can record a large amount of information, personal or business, for the entries in the Contacts record.

To open the Contacts folder, select People on the Shortcuts bar.

Double-click an entry to open it and review or amend the details. You can record a large amount of information, personal or business, for the entries in your Contacts folder.

159

Spam and Phishing

While very useful, email does have problem areas. Because it is so cheap and easy to use, the criminally inclined take advantage. They send out thousands of spam (junk email) messages, in the hope of getting one or two replies.

Beware

Don't respond in any way to messages that you think may be spam. Even clicking on an Unsubscribe link will confirm that your address is a genuine email account, and this may get it added to lists of validated account names.

Hot tip

Any message sent to the Junk Email folder is converted to plain-text format, and all links are disabled. In addition, the Reply and Reply All functions are disabled.

> ⓘ Links and other functionality have been disabled in this message. To turn on that functionality, move this message to the Inbox.

Don't forget

You can block messages from specified top level domain codes, and messages in particular foreign languages.

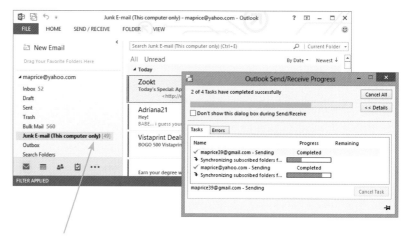

The Outlook Junk Email filter identifies spam as messages are received, and moves the invalid messages to the Junk Email folder. To adjust the settings:

1. From the Home tab, select the Junk button in the Delete group, then click Junk Email Options...

2. Select your desired level of protection: No Automatic Filtering, Low (default), High or Safe Lists Only

3. Click the related tab, to specify lists of safe senders, safe recipients or blocked senders and international domains

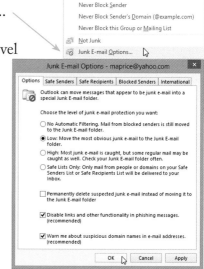

Outlook also provides protection from your Inbox messages.

1 Links to pictures on the sender's website may be blocked, links to websites may be disabled, and the Reply and Reply All functions may be made inactive

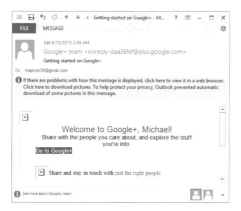

To explore how Outlook handles potentially damaging messages, visit the website **www.emailsecuritycheck.net/** Submit an email address, and respond to the confirming email.

Review the subsequent emails you receive from this website to see how Outlook responds to the various scenarios.

For example, Outlook blocks access to an attachment that's executable and so potentially dangerous.

Hot tip

Links to pictures and other content from a website may be blocked, since these are sometimes the source of viruses and other threats. Only download them if you trust the sender.

Beware

Some spam messages and websites try to trick you into providing passwords, PINs, and personal details. Referred to as phishing (pronounced fishing),they appear to be from well-known organizations, such as banks and charities.

Don't forget

The attachments and links in these test emails are innocuous, but do illustrate ways in which the security of your system could be impacted.

Create a Message

Hot tip

You can also select New Email message from the Jump list, which appears when you right-click the program entry on the taskbar (or click the program entry pinned to the Start menu).

Don't forget

You can send the same message to more than one addressee. You can also select addressees for the Cc (courtesy copy) or Bcc (blind courtesy copy) options.

1 Select the Mail folder, and then click the New button to open a mail message form

2 Click the To button to open the address book and list your contacts

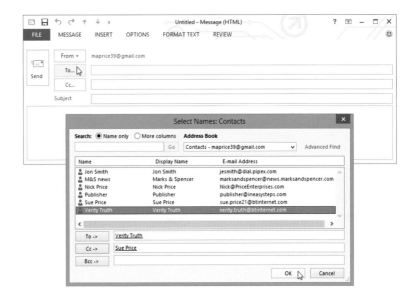

3 Select the addressee and click To, then add any other addressees and then click OK

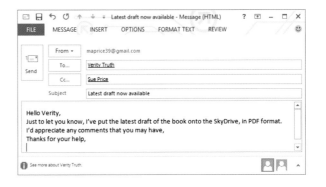

4 Type the subject, the greeting, and the content text for your message

Insert a Signature

You can create a standard signature block, to add to the emails you send.

1 Select the Insert tab and click Signature in the Include group, then click Signatures

2 Click the New button, specify a name for the new signature, then click OK

Hot tip

The first time you select the Signature button, there'll be no signatures defined, so you must start off by creating one.

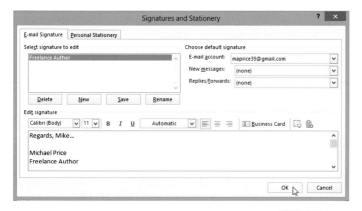

Don't forget

You can specify one of your signatures as the default for new messages, or for replies and forwards, and the appropriate signature will be automatically applied for future messages.

3 Add the text required, and click OK to save the signature

4 When you've added one or more, click Signature again and select a signature to add to the message, at the typing cursor location

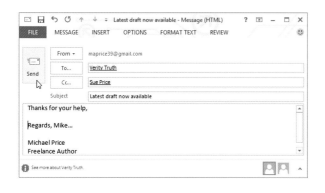

Don't forget

Click the Send button to store the message in the Outbox, ready for the next Send. Click the Send/Receive tab and select Send/Receive to send immediately.

Message Tags

You use tags to help sort and organize messages.

1 Select a message from a POP3 connection (see page 150) and select the Home tab

2 Click Unread/Read to toggle the read status of the selected message

Hot tip

Email accounts that use an IMAP connection do not have the Categorize tag for their messages. Also, Follow Up is limited to a simple flag.

3 Click Categorize to choose a color to associate with the selected message

4 The first time you select a specific color, you have the option to rename it, or assign it a shortcut key

Don't forget

Choose Set Quick Click, to define the color category to be assigned when you single-click the Categories column.

5 The Categories column is added to the message details, and this field can be used to group messages

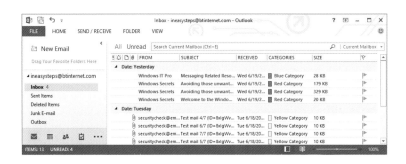

Hot tip

You can select from a variety of predefined reminder notes.

```
Call
Do not Forward
Follow up
For Your Information
Forward
No Response Necessary
Read
Reply
Reply to All
Review
```

6 Click Follow Up to assign a flag to the selected message

7 Select the appropriate flag, or add a To-Do item as a reminder

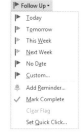

RSS Feeds

RSS (Really Simple Syndication) is a way for publishers of Internet data to make news, blogs, and other information available to subscribers. You can add feeds and view subscriptions in either Internet Explorer or Outlook.

To synchronize these programs:

1. Identify an RSS feed on a website by one of these active icons on the Command bar

2. Click the down arrow next to the icon and select one of the feeds offered

3. Click Subscribe to this feed, then click the Subscribe button to confirm

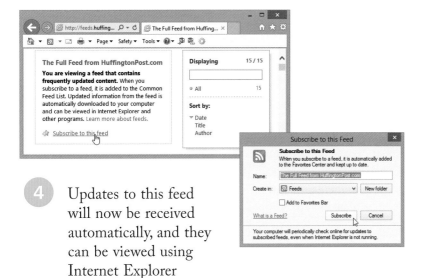

4. Updates to this feed will now be received automatically, and they can be viewed using Internet Explorer

Hot tip

Subscribing to RSS feeds from Internet Explorer is the quickest and easiest way to add RSS feeds to Outlook.

Hot tip

The RSS feeds you subscribe to using Internet Explorer are added to the Common Feed List and can be viewed using Outlook (see page 166).

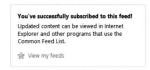

...cont'd

Hot tip

When you subscribe to RSS feeds from Internet Explorer, you can use Outlook to view the updates as they arrive.

To synchronize the RSS feeds and subscriptions in Outlook with those in Internet Explorer:

1 Click File, Open & Import, Import/Export, select RSS Feeds from the Common Feed List, Next

2 Select individual feeds to add to Outlook (or click the Select All button) and click Next, and Finish

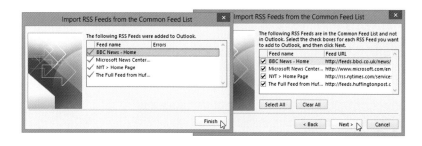

Don't forget

To ensure that the programs remain synchronized, select File, Options, Advanced, and then Synchronize RSS Feeds.

3 Select RSS Feeds in the Outlook Folders pane to view the updates

9 Time Management

Outlook is a complete personal information management system, with full diary and calendar facilities. It enables you to keep track of appointments and meetings, and to control and schedule your tasks. You can keep notes, make journal entries, and correlate all these with email messages relating to those records.

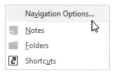

To replace folder names by their associated icons, click the ••• dots and then Navigation Options.

Adjust the number of items displayed and their display sequence, then click in the box for Compact Navigation.

Outlook Today displays a summary of the calendar activities, the tasks, and the counts of unread messages on your system. Click the Calendar header to display the full calendar.

Outlook Calendar

Outlook Calendar handles time-based activities, including appointments, meetings, holidays, courses, and events. It provides a high-level view by day, week, or month and gives reminders when activities are due. To open:

1 Click the Calendar button on the Navigation bar

Date navigator   Time bar   View   Events   Meeting

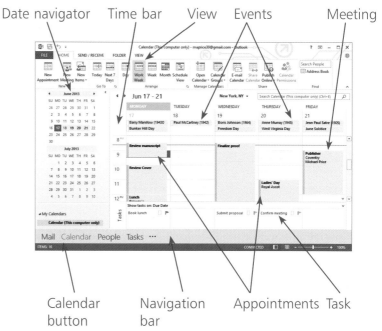

Calendar   Navigation   Appointments Task
button   bar

You also see current calendar events on the Today page:

1 Click the Mail icon and select your email account

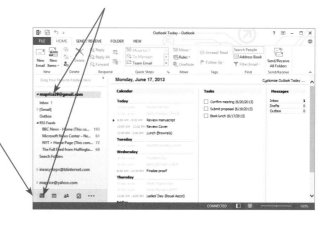

Schedule an Appointment

An appointment reserves space in your calendar for an
activity or for a resource, without inviting other people.

1 Open the Calendar (day, week, or month view) and
use the date navigator to select the appointment day

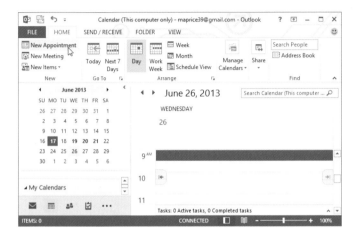

You can also double-
click the Start time
area, or right-click the
area and select New
Appointment.

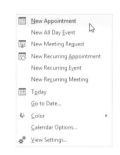

2 Using the mouse pointer, select the start time for the
appointment, then click New Appointment button

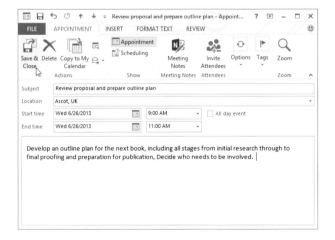

To change the End
time and duration,
click the down-arrow
and select a new
value. You can also
change the Start time
(the current duration
will be maintained).

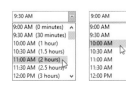

3 Type the subject, then select the end time, enter
any other details you have, such as Location and
Description, then select the Save & Close button

Change Appointment Details

The appointment is added to the calendar, which shows the subject, start time, duration and location. Move the mouse over the appointment area to see more details.

Don't forget

Single-click the calendar at the appointment area and you can edit the text of the subject title. Double-click the area and you will open the appointment for edit.

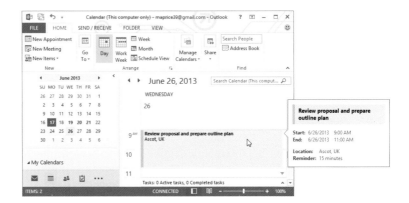

1 Select the appointment and the Calendar Tools tab is added, with related options displayed on the Ribbon

Hot tip

By default, you will get a reminder pop up for the appointment 15 minutes before the start time, or you can set your own notice period (values between zero and two weeks), or turn off the reminder.

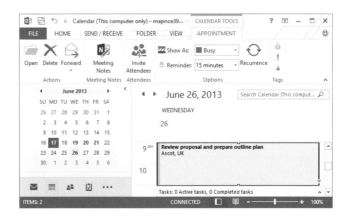

2 Click Open or double-click the appointment to open the appointment editor form (see page 169), add or change any of the details and click Save & Close)

3 To change the start or finish times move the mouse pointer to the top or bottom edge and drag it to the required time. The duration changes to match

Recurring Appointments

When you have an activity that's repeated on a regular basis, you can define it as a recurring appointment.

1 Open the appointments form, specify the details for a first occurrence of the activity, and click Recurrence

You can take an existing appointment, or meeting, and click Recurrence to make it a recurring activity.

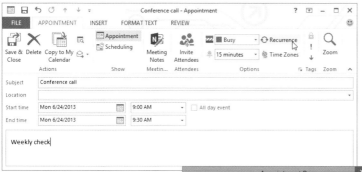

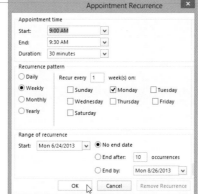

2 Specify how often the activity will be repeated, and over what range of time it should take place

3 Click OK, and click Save & Close to record the changes

Unless you limit the number of recurrences, or set a termination date, the activity will be scheduled for all possible days in the future.

Depending on the view chosen and the space available, the recurrence symbol may appear after the subject in each entry.

4 All the occurrences will be displayed in the calendar

9 Conference call

Create a Meeting

Hot tip

You convert an existing appointment into a meeting, by defining the attendees and sending invitations.

1 Double-click the appointment entry in the calendar, and click the Invite Attendees button in the Attendees group

2 On the invitation message form displayed, click the To button to open the contacts address list

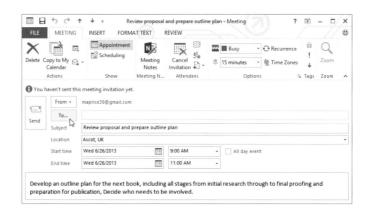

Don't forget

You can also schedule meeting resources, such as rooms, screens, and projectors.

3 Select the email address for each attendee in turn, and click Required or Optional as appropriate. Click OK when you've added all attendees

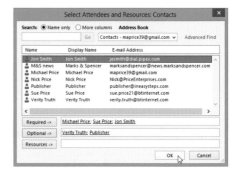

4 When all the attendees have been added, click the Send button to send the invitation to each of them

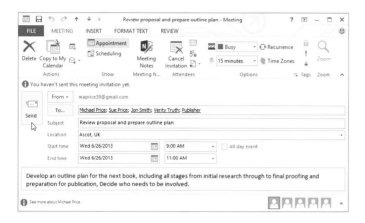

5 The invitation is received in the organizer's Inbox

You can double-click the meeting entry in your calendar to view the current status, which will initially show No responses have been received for this meeting.

6 There's no response required from the organizer

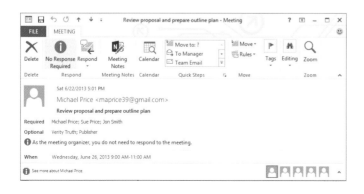

Respond to an Invitation

The attendees must be using a version of Outlook in order to be able to properly receive and respond to meeting invitations.

You can click the Tentative button to accept provisionally.

You can edit the response, if desired, or you can accept the invitation without sending a response. It will simply be added to your calendar.

1 The other attendees receive and open the invitation, and see buttons to accept or decline, or change the time

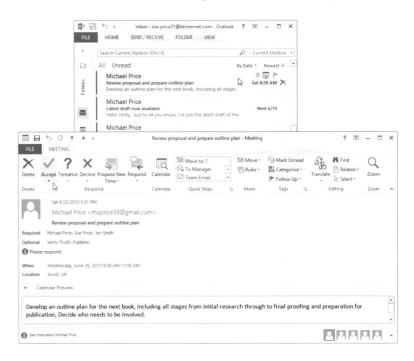

2 Click Accept, then select Send the Response Now, to add the appointment to your calendar

3 The original message is removed from the Inbox, and the response is inserted into the Sent box

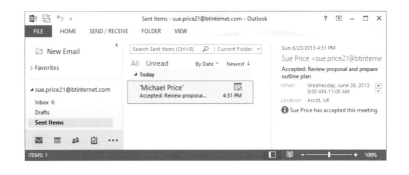

4 The originator gets email responses from attendees

The message shows the current status, so it will show the latest information each time it is opened.

5 The message shows the attendee's response and status

6 The meeting record displays the updated status

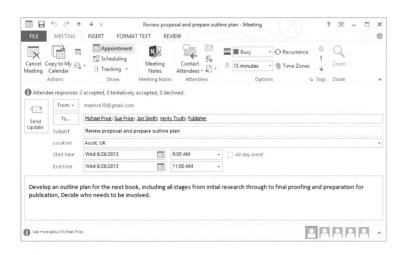

Any changes that the originator makes to the meeting details will be sent to the attendees as update messages.

Add Holidays

To make sure that your calendar is an accurate reflection of your availability, add details of national holidays and events.

Hot tip

By default, no holidays or special events are shown in your Calendar, but Outlook does have a holiday file, with information for 112 countries and events for the years 2012-2022.

1 Open Outlook, select File and then Options

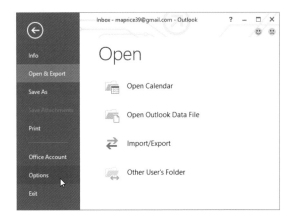

2 In Outlook Options, select Calendar then click the Add Holidays button in the Calendar options

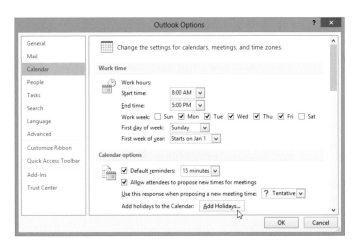

Don't forget

Your own country or region is automatically selected each time you choose the Add Holidays option.

3 Select the country or countries that you wish to add, for example the United Kingdom and the United States, then click OK

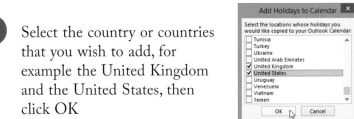

...cont'd

4 The entries for the selected countries are imported

Don't forget

Your own country or region is automatically selected each time you choose the Add Holidays option.

5 Click OK when holidays have been added then click OK to leave the Options

To see the new entries in the calendar:

1 Open the Calendar, select the View tab and click Change View

2 Select the List option and the calendar contents are displayed in Start date order

177

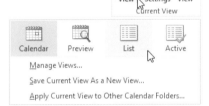

Hot tip

If you have more than one country inserted, you can click Location to Group By This Field. Use this, for example, to remove the events for one country.

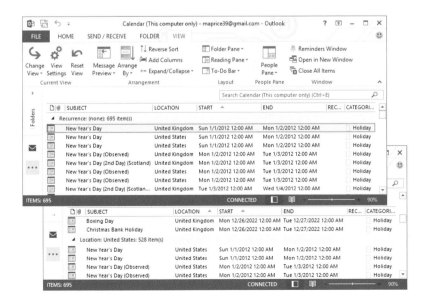

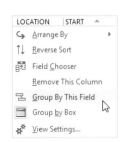

Sharing free/busy information works best on systems that use a Microsoft Exchange email server. Other email systems may require you to Import the busy information (see page 179).

Don't forget

You could also set up a calendars and free/busy reports to coordinate the use of resources such as conference rooms and projector equipment.

Report Free/Busy Time

Outlook can help you choose the most suitable times to hold meetings, based on reports from the proposed attendees, giving details of their availability.

To set up a procedure for publishing this information, each potential attendee should:

1 Open Outlook and select File, Options, Calendar

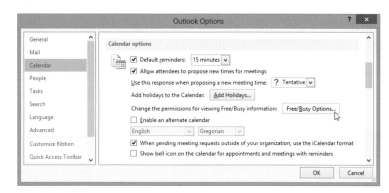

2 Click Free/Busy Options in the Calendar Options

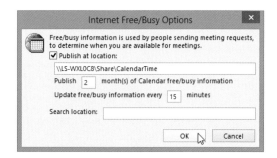

3 Click the box for Publish at location, and provide the address for a networked folder or drive that is accessible by all potential attendees, then click OK

The free/busy data for the specified period (e.g. 2 months) and will be updated regularly (e.g. every 15 minutes). It will be stored at the location defined, in the form of username. vbf files (using the username from the attendee's email ID).

Schedule a Meeting

You can use the reported free/busy information to help set up a meeting. For example, to schedule a new meeting:

1 Create the meeting (see page 172) with details, such as expected start, duration, and proposed attendees

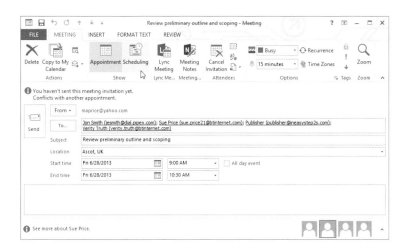

2 Click Scheduling, to show free/busy times, and click AutoPick Next to see the next available time slot

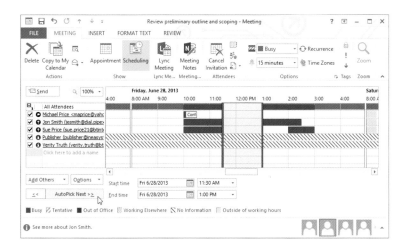

3 Click Send to add revised details to your calendar, and send an invitation (or an update) to all attendees

You can then select File, Open & Export and then Import/ Export to import their saved calendars and add their busy times to your calendar, ready to schedule the meeting.

Creating Tasks

Hot tip

Outlook can create and manage implicit tasks (as follow-ups of other Outlook items). It can also create explicit tasks, which can be assigned to others. To display the Task folder, click the ··· dots on the Navigation bar and select Tasks.

To create an implicit task:

1 Right-click an Outlook item (for example, a message or contact), select Follow Up and select the flag for the timing

2 The follow-up item is added to the Task folder, and also appears on the To-Do bar

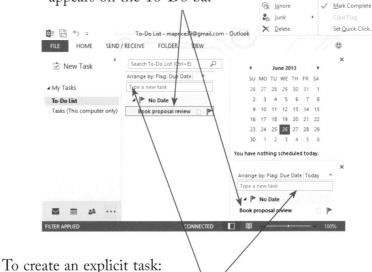

To create an explicit task:

1 Click the prompt "Type a new task" in the Task folder, or on the To-Do bar

2 Type the subject for the task, and then press Enter

3 The task is inserted into the Tasks folder, with the default characteristics (current date for the start date and the due date, and with no reminder time set)

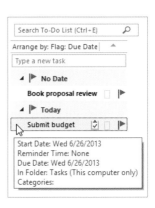

Don't forget

This provides a quick way to generate a To-Do list of actions. Note that an entry changes color, to red, when its due date has passed.

...cont'd

To make changes to details for the task:

1 Double-click the task entry on the To-Do bar, or in the Task folder

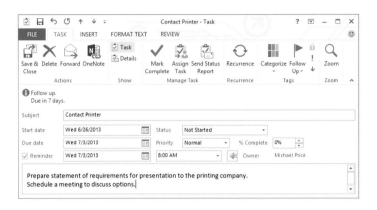

2 You can change the start date or the due date, add a description, apply a reminder, update the priority, or indicate how much has been completed

3 When you update the % Complete, the status changes to In progress or Complete, or you can click the down-arrow to choose an alternative status

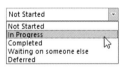

4 Click the Details button in the Show group to add information about task activity, e.g. hours worked

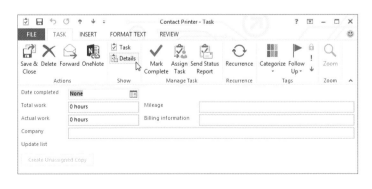

As with the editors for other Outlook items, the Task editor uses the Ribbon technology.

Click the arrows on the % Complete box to increase or decrease by 25% at a time, or type an exact percentage in the box.

Click Save & Close, in Task or Details view, to record the changes.

Assigning Tasks

You can define a task that someone else is to perform, assign it to that person and get status reports and progress updates.

To assign an existing task:

1 Open the task and click Assign Task, in the Manage Task

Hot tip

To create and assign a new task, select New and Task Request from the menu bar, or press Ctrl + Shift + U. Then enter the subject and other task details, along with the assignee name.

182

Don't forget

Select or clear the boxes for Keep an updated copy of this task on my task list and Send me a status report when this task is complete, as desired.

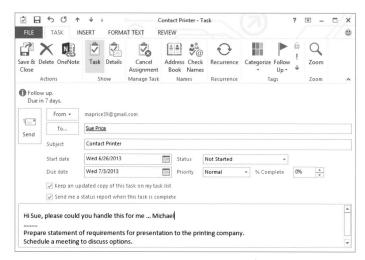

2 In the To box, type the name or email address for the assignee, or click the To button and select an entry from the Contacts list

3 Click Send, to initiate the task-assignment request, then click OK to confirm the new ownership

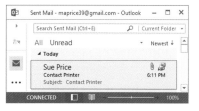

4 The message will be sent to the assignee, with a copy stored in the Sent Items folder

Accepting Task Requests

1 The task details on the originating system show it is awaiting a response from the recipient of the request

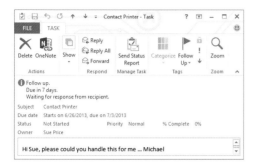

2 The task request appears in the recipient's Inbox

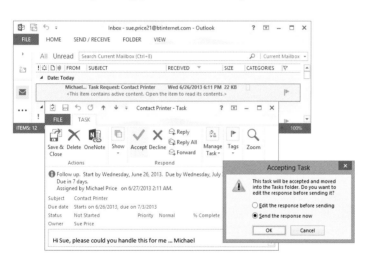

Hot tip

If the task is rejected, ownership is returned to the originator, who can then assign the task to another person.

3 The recipient opens the message, clicks the Accept button, then clicks OK to send the response

Don't forget

The task request is sent to the originator, and a copy is saved in the Sent Items folder.

Confirming the Assignment

1 The response appears in the originator's Inbox, as a message from the recipient of the task request

2 When the message is opened, it shows the task with its change of ownership

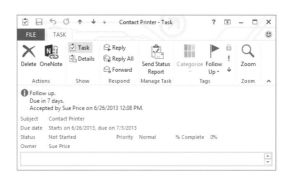

The originator is no longer able to make changes to the task details, since ownership has been transferred to the recipient.

3 The task appears in the originator's Tasks folder, grouped under the new owner's name

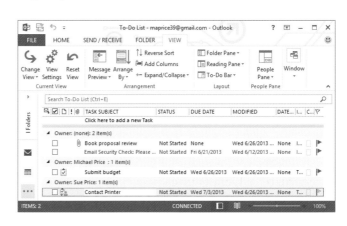

4 The new owner can change task details, and click Save & Close to save them, as the task progresses

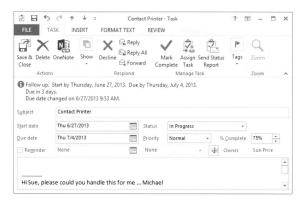

When the recipient makes any changes to the task details, messages are sent to the originator, to update the entry in the task folder.

5 For each change, the originator is sent an update message, to change the task details in the task folder

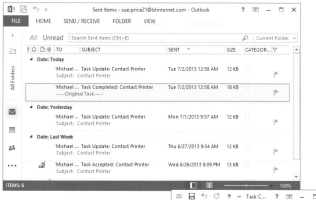

6 When the task is finally completed, the originator receives a status report

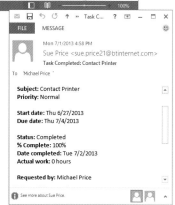

Click the message box to list all related messages, in the Inbox or Sent Items folders.

7 Note that hours worked will only be shown if recorded in Details (see page 181)

Notes

You may need a prompt for an activity that doesn't justify a task or an appointment. In such a case, you can use Outlook Notes. To create a note from anywhere in Outlook:

Hot tip

Outlook Notes are the electronic equivalent of sticky notes, and they can be used for anything you need to remember.

1 Press shortcut Ctrl + Shift + N

2 Type the text for your note in the form that's displayed, and it is added to the Notes folder

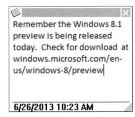

Remember the Windows 8.1 preview is being released today. Check for download at windows.microsoft.com/en-us/windows-8/preview

6/26/2013 10:23 AM

3 Click the ··· dots on the Navigation bar and select Notes to see the current set of notes stored in that folder

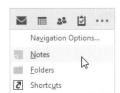

Navigation Options...
Notes
Folders
Shortcuts

Don't forget

You can leave the note open, or click the [X] Close button. In either case, there's no need to save the note – it is recorded automatically.

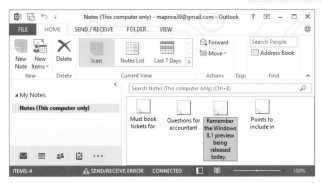

4 The note titles may be truncated, so select a note to see its full title – the text up to the first Enter, or else the whole text, if there's no Enter symbol

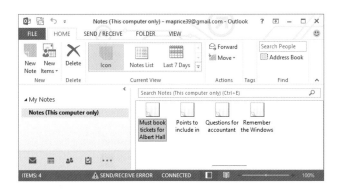

...cont'd

5 Select the View tab and click List (or Small Icons) to allow more space for the note titles

Don't forget

The notes are of a standard size, but you can click and drag an edge or a corner to make a note any size you wish.

6 Right-click a note to copy, to print, to forward to another user, or to delete it

You can resize notes.

6/27/2013 11:59 AM

To change the view settings for your Notes folder:

1 Select the View tab then click View Settings to adjust Sort or Filter options

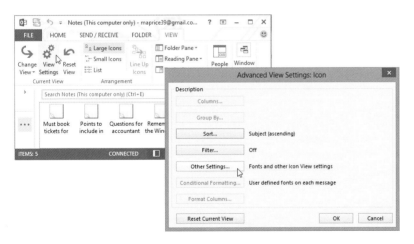

2 Click Other Settings to adjust the options that manage the icon placement

Hot tip

The settings for the Icon view are shown. There'll be a different set of options available if you choose the Notes List or the Last 7 Days views.

Beware

The Journal has been reduced in function in Office 2013, so consider other methods for managing activities, for example, using Tasks.

Don't forget

You can select from a wide variety of Journal entry types.

Conversation
Document
E-mail Message
Fax
Letter
Meeting
Meeting cancellation
Meeting request
Meeting response
Microsoft Excel
Microsoft Office Access
Microsoft PowerPoint
Microsoft Word
Note
Phone call
Remote session
Task
Task request
Task response

Hot tip

You can drag & drop items from Mail, Calendar and other Outlook folders to add them to the Journal.

Journal

You can record information about activities related to Outlook items in the Journal, a type of project log book.

1 Click ⋯ on the Navigation bar and select Folders, then select Journal from the Folders pane

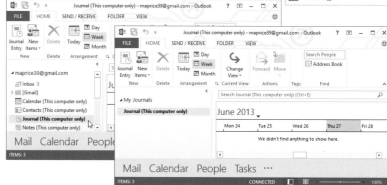

2 Alternatively, press shortcut key Ctrl + 8 to open the Journal directly

3 Select Journal Entry to create a new item

4 Enter the details then click Save & Close

5 The entries appear on a Timeline

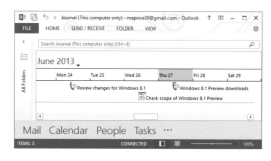

10 Manage Files and Fonts

It is useful to understand how Office stores and manages the files and fonts that make up your documents, so that you can choose the best formats when you share documents with others over the Internet.

Windows Version

Although most features of Office 2013 are independent of the actual version of Windows you are using, there are differences to watch out for, when starting any of the Office applications and managing the associated files and folders.

To illustrate the differences:

1 In **Windows 7**, select Start, More Programs then double-click Office 2013

2 Select Word 2013 from the Office 2013 folder

3 From Word 2013 select File and then click Open

4 Choose the file location, for example Computer, My Documents to access your Documents library then choose a document, e.g. Overview

These screenshots show the use of the Start menu to open applications, and also illustrate the use of the Windows 7 Aero Glass theme, which provides transparency effects.

Hot tip

Despite the switch from Start menu to Start screen and contrasts in style between Windows 7 and Windows 8, most operations in Office 2013 will be the same. However, there are some differences in the ways that you manage files.

Don't forget

If your system uses the Home Basic edition of Windows 7, this is functionally the same, but does not display the Aero Glass transparency effects.

...cont'd

1 In **Windows 8**, display the Start screen to click the Word 2013 tile

2 Alternatively, select Desktop from the Start screen and click the Word 2013 icon on the Taskbar

3 From Word 2013 select File and then click Open

If the Taskbar does not show a shortcut for a particular application, you can right-click its tile on the Start screen and select Pin to Taskbar.

Don't forget

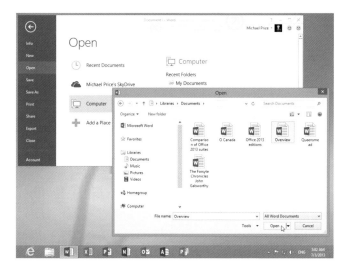

4 Choose the file location and locate the document you want to open, e.g. My Documents and Overview

This shows how you open applications in Windows 8. There is no Aero Glass effect in this version of Windows, but the contents of the windows and the functions offered are just the same as those provided in the Windows 7 environment.

In both cases, the option is offered to Search Documents, to help you locate documents by name or by content.

Hot tip

When you select My Documents, you access the Documents library for the current user, just as in Windows 7, but the File Explorer window does not choose to highlight this aspect.

Library Location

To see where your library of documents is located:

1 In the Open window, select the Documents library in the Navigation pane and click the triangle to expand it (or simply double-click Documents)

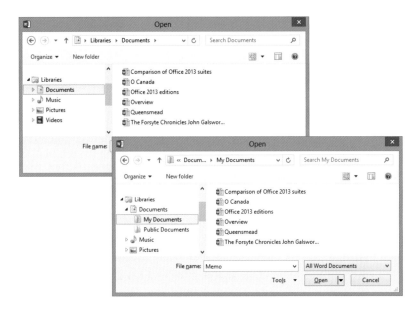

2 Select the My Documents location that's displayed and you'll see the documents shown in the library

3 Click the address area and it is converted into drive address format, showing that the user's documents are in the folder C:\Users\username\documents

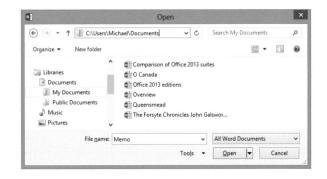

Finding Files

The search facilities are strengths of Windows 7 or 8, and Office 2013 takes full advantage of them. To illustrate this, suppose you create a document discussing the Stayman bridge convention, but happen to save it in the wrong folder.

To track it down, when using Office 2013 with Windows 8:

1 Open Word 2013 and select File, Open, then choose the starting location e.g. Computer, My Documents

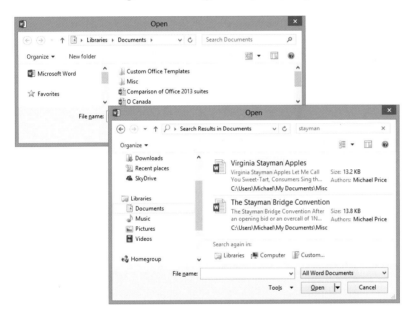

193

2 Click in the Search box, and type the search terms, e.g., Stayman. Matching documents from the starting location and its subfolders are displayed immediately

3 Select the Content view to see details of the files, including parts of the text and the full path

4 Right-click a file, and select Open file location, to see the folder where it is stored. Double-click the file to open it in Word and view or edit its contents

Select Documents, or choose another folder or drive where you expect to find your missing document.

This shows that the required document has been misfiled in the Misc folder within Documents. You'll get similar results using Windows 7.

Any documents that contain the specified word in their titles, or in their contents, will be selected.

...cont'd

Don't forget

Although Word is used in these examples, the same search procedures apply for documents in other Office applications, for example, Excel and PowerPoint.

To locate documents using operating system search facilities:

1 In Windows 7, click the Start button and simply type the search term, e.g. stayman

2 Matching documents, applications and other files are identified and listed so you can locate or open them

Don't forget

Hold the mouse pointer over a search result, and the ToolTip will show the location where the file or document is stored.

3 In Windows 8, display the Start screen and simply type the search term to automatically invoke Search

4 Windows 8 counts matches for Apps, Settings and Files, lists only Apps. Click another set if needed

Recent Documents

When you want to return to a document you worked with earlier, you may find it in the recently-used documents list.

1 Select File, Open and click Recent Documents and click an entry in the documents list to open it

Beware

If a document is moved or renamed, the entry in Recent Documents is not updated, so it will give an error indicating Document not found.

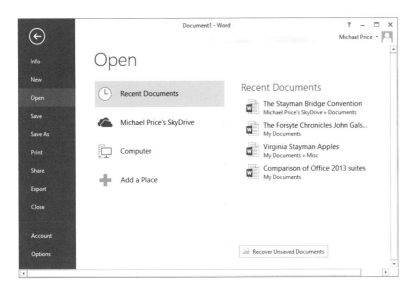

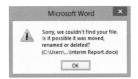

2 You can right-click the application icon on the Taskbar to display the Jump list with Recent items

Hot tip

Right-click on an unwanted item, and select Remove from list. Choose Clear unpinned Documents, to remove all the items.

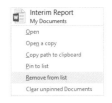

Windows 7

In Windows 7, you can select an application on the Start menu to see a list of its recent items.

The Start menu may also offer the Recent Items entry which lists files for several applications, for example Word, Excel and PowerPoint.

Change File Type

To change the file types listed when you open documents:

Hot tip

Showing additional file types will make it easier to locate the correct document, when you use a variety of file types in your applications.

1 From Word 2013, select the File tab, click Open and select the file location, e.g. My Documents\Misc

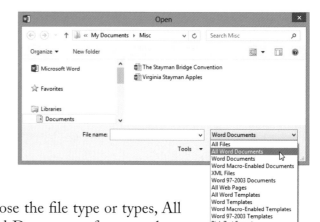

2 Choose the file type or types, All Word Documents, for example

3 Files of the specified type are listed

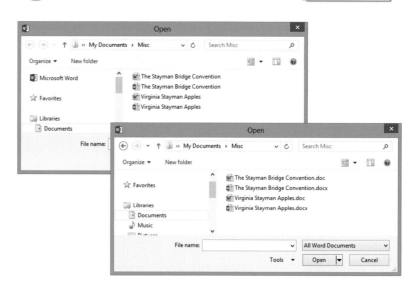

Don't forget

You can have more than one document with the same name, but different file extensions, if you have, for example, Office 2013 and Office 2003 versions.

4 You must change folder views in File Explorer (see page 24) to show the file name extensions

XML File Formats

Office 2013 uses file formats based on XML. They apply to Word 2013, Excel 2013, PowerPoint 2013 and Visio 2013. The XML file types include:

Application	XML file type	Extension
Word	Document	.docx
	Macro-enabled document	.docm
	Template	.dotx
	Macro-enabled template	.dotm
Excel	Workbook	.xlsx
	Macro-enabled workbook	.xlsm
	Template	.xltx
	Macro-enabled template	.xltm
	Non-XML binary workbook	.xlsb
	Macro-enabled add-in	.xlam
PowerPoint	Presentation	.pptx
	Macro-enabled presentation	.pptm
	Template	.potx
	Macro-enabled template	.potm
	Macro-enabled add-in	.ppam
	Show	.ppsx
	Macro-enabled show	.ppsm
Visio	Drawing	.vsdx
	Macro-enabled drawing	.vsdm
	Stencil	.vssx
	Macro-enabled stencil	.vssm
	Template	.vstx
	Macro-enabled template	.vstm

The XML formats are automatically compressed, and can be up to 75% smaller, saving disk space and reducing transmission times when you send files via email or the Web. Files are structured in a modular fashion, which allows files to be opened, even if a component within the file (for example, a chart or table) is damaged or corrupted (see page 204).

The .docx, .xlsx and .pptx file format extensions are also used for the Strict Open XML formats, which are ISO versions of the XML formats.

This is all handled automatically. You do not have to install any special zip utilities to open and close files in Office 2013.

Save As PDF or XPS

There are times when you'd like to allow other users to view and print your documents, but you'd rather they didn't make changes. These could include résumés, legal documents, newsletters, or any documents meant for review only. Office 2013 provides for this with two built-in file formats.

Portable Document Format (PDF)

PDF is a fixed-layout file format that preserves your document formatting when the file is viewed online or printed, while the data in the file cannot be easily changed. The PDF format is also useful for commercial printing methods.

XML Paper Specification (XPS)

XPS also preserves document formatting and protects the data content. However, it is not yet widely used. The XPS format ensures that, when the file is viewed online or printed, it retains the exact format you intended, and that data in the file cannot be easily changed.

To save an Office document in either format:

1 Open the document in the appropriate application, for example, open a document using Word 2013

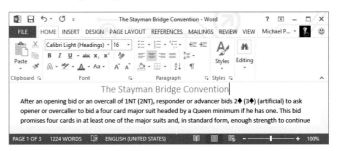

2 Make final changes to the document, then select the File tab and click Save

3 Select the location to store the new copy. The default is the current folder, in this case in My Documents\Misc

4 Click the Save as type box, and select PDF or XPS

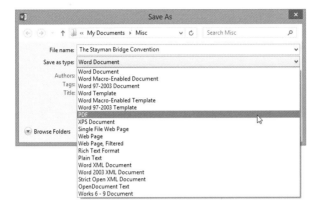

5 Select Standard or Online quality, and click Save

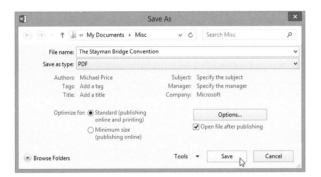

6 The document is saved to disk in the required format, and then displayed using the Microsoft Reader app, which supports both PDF and XPS

Fonts in Office 2013

There are a number of fonts provided with Office 2013, such as Calibri, Comic Sans, Gabriola, Georgia, Impact and Verdana. Preview text using these and other Windows fonts:

1 From the Home tab, select the text to be previewed, click the down-arrow on the Font box

Calibri is the default font for Office 2013, replacing the Times New Roman font that was used in earlier versions of Office.

2 Scroll the list to locate an interesting font, then move the mouse pointer over the font name to see an immediate preview using that font

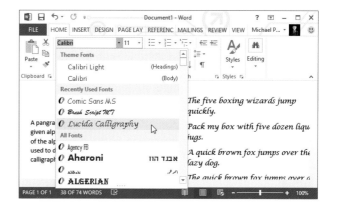

The font sample box usually extends over the text, hiding much of the preview. It can be dragged up to reveal more of the text, but will then display fewer fonts.

3 Click on the desired font name to apply the change

This helps indicate how the text will appear, but it is an awkward way to explore the large number of fonts available.

...cont'd

Using a macro from Microsoft, you can create a document that provides a sample of every font on your system.

1 Visit **support.microsoft.com/kb/209205**

Hot tip

There are two macros. ListFonts creates a document with samples for each font. ListAllFonts provides similar content, but uses a table format.

2 Scroll down to ListAllFonts, and select the code

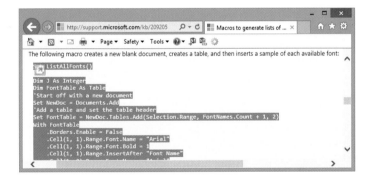

Don't forget

Highlight all the lines of code, ready for copying, from the first line:

    Sub ListAllFonts()

to the last line:

    End Sub

3 Open a new blank document, and select the View tab, ready to work with macros

Create and Run ListAllFonts

1 Click the arrow on the Macros button in the Macros group, and select the View Macros entry

2 Name the macro ListAllFonts, choose Macros in Document1, and click Create

3 Highlight the skeleton code to replace it

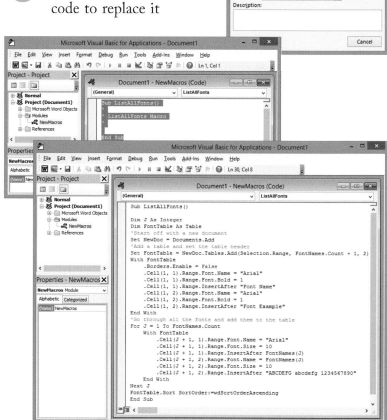

```
Sub ListAllFonts()

Dim J As Integer
Dim FontTable As Table
'Start off with a new document
Set NewDoc = Documents.Add
'Add a table and set the table header
Set FontTable = NewDoc.Tables.Add(Selection.Range, FontNames.Count + 1, 2)
With FontTable
    .Borders.Enable = False
    .Cell(1, 1).Range.Font.Name = "Arial"
    .Cell(1, 1).Range.Font.Bold = 1
    .Cell(1, 1).Range.InsertAfter "Font Name"
    .Cell(1, 2).Range.Font.Name = "Arial"
    .Cell(1, 2).Range.Font.Bold = 1
    .Cell(1, 2).Range.InsertAfter "Font Example"
End With
'Go through all the fonts and add them to the table
For J = 1 To FontNames.Count
    With FontTable
        .Cell(J + 1, 1).Range.Font.Name = "Arial"
        .Cell(J + 1, 1).Range.Font.Size = 10
        .Cell(J + 1, 1).Range.InsertAfter FontNames(J)
        .Cell(J + 1, 2).Range.Font.Name = FontNames(J)
        .Cell(J + 1, 2).Range.Font.Size = 10
        .Cell(J + 1, 2).Range.InsertAfter "ABCDEFG abcdefg 1234567890"
    End With
Next J
FontTable.Sort SortOrder:=wdSortOrderAscending
End Sub
```

4 Copy and paste the code from the Microsoft website, then select File, Close and Return to Microsoft Word

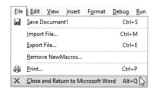

5 Reselect View Macros, click the macro name ListAllFonts, and then click Run

6 A new document is created, and the font names and examples are displayed as a table

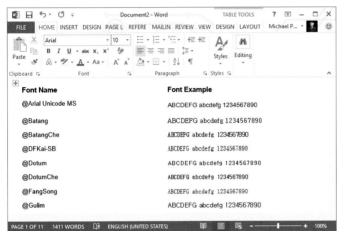

Font Name	Font Example
@Arial Unicode MS	ABCDEFG abcdefg 1234567890
@Batang	ABCDEFG abcdefg 1234567890
@BatangChe	ABCDEFG abcdefg 1234567890
@DFKai-SB	ABCDEFG abcdefg 1234567890
@Dotum	ABCDEFG abcdefg 1234567890
@DotumChe	ABCDEFG abcdefg 1234567890
@FangSong	ABCDEFG abcdefg 1234567890
@Gulim	ABCDEFG abcdefg 1234567890

7 Save the new document, to keep the table of font names and examples for future reference. Save the first document to retain the ListAllFonts macro

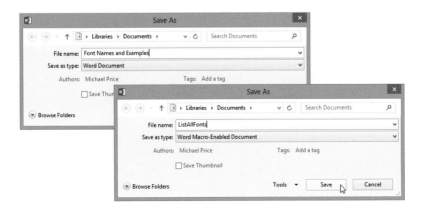

Hot tip

You can use your own text for the samples, by changing code line: Cell(J + 1, 2).Range. InsertAfter "ABCDEFG abcdefg 1234567890".

203

Don't forget

The macro is created in the first document, which can be closed without saving. It is not required to view the font samples in the second document. However, if you do want to save the original document, you must make it a macro-enabled document.

Document Recovery

Sometimes your system may, for one reason or another, close down before you have saved the changes to the document you were working on. The next time you start the application concerned, the Document Recovery feature will recover as much of the work you'd carried out as possible since the last save.

1 Open the program (e.g. Word) and click Show Recovered Documents

If a program freezes, you may have to force Logoff, or Shutdown without being able to save your document.

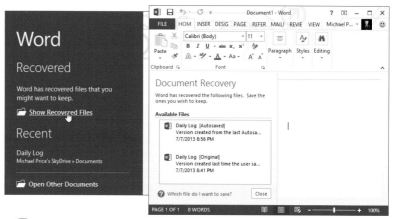

2 Check the versions of the document that are offered, and choose the one closest to your requirements

3 Select File, Save As, rename and save the document

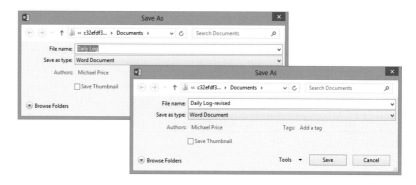

By default, documents are autosaved every ten minutes, but you can adjust the timing (see page 32).

Provide a different name for the autosaved version, "Daily Log-revised" for example, if you want to retain the original.

11 Up-to-Date and Secure

Microsoft Update makes sure that you take advantage of updates to Office. Online Help gives you the latest advice and guidance. Office also enables you to protect your documents, control access to them and secure your system.

Enable Updates

1 The first time you run an Office 2013 application you'll be asked to choose your preferred settings

Don't forget

After you install Office 2013 and run any of the applications for the first time, you will be asked to Activate your copy of Office and then choose the settings for Update.

The recommended settings will provide you with updates for Office, Windows, and other Microsoft software, together with various problem-solving facilities. Alternatively, you can choose to install updates only.

You can choose not to apply updates, though this can leave your computer open to security threats. However, you can change the update settings at a later date:

Hot tip

In Windows 7, select the Start button then click Control Panel on the Start menu. In Windows 8, switch to the Desktop, display the Charms bar, click Settings and then select Control Panel.

1 Open the Control Panel and select System and Security, Windows Update

2 For updates for Office 2013 and other Microsoft products, click Find out more

...cont'd

3 The Windows Update web page opens. Agree the Terms of Use and click the Install button

Don't forget

There's a similar process for updating Office 2013, and other Microsoft software running under Windows 7.

4 Microsoft Update is installed and you are reminded how to find Windows Update from the Start screen

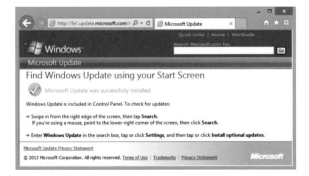

5 With the revised settings, Windows Update checks for updates for Windows, Office and other products

Hot tip

Windows Update will in future automatically check for updates, and will also automatically install them.

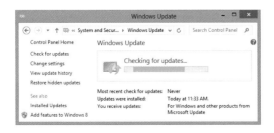

Apply Updates

1 Windows Update tells you the number of updates

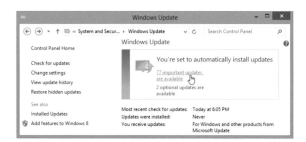

2 To see details, click the link with the number found

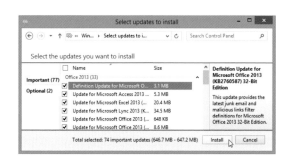

Hot tip

You can select the View Update History link to see details of the updates that have been applied.

3 Windows Update installs the updates automatically, or you can click the Install button to install them immediately

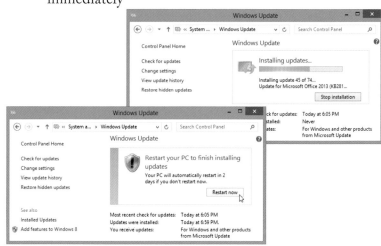

Don't forget

When updating has been completed, you may be prompted to restart the system to fully apply all the updates.

Change Settings

To view and change the settings for Windows Update:

1 Open Windows Update from the Control Panel (or find it from the Start screen - see page 207)

In Windows 7, you can select Start, All Programs and find an entry for Windows Update on the Start menu.

2 Select Change Settings to view or change values

3 Review the details for the update action, including the time of day assigned for scheduled maintenance

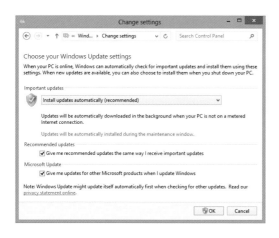

Windows Update will schedule updates daily at the specified time, as long as the computer is not otherwise busy.

Office Help

There are two ways to display the Office Help for an application. With the application open:

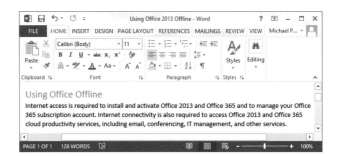

Hot tip

You invoke Office Help in the same way in each Office application, though the Help window that opens is specific to the active application, in this case, Word. The layout is similar for all the Office applications.

1 Press the F1 shortcut on the keyboard

2 Click the **?** icon at the right of the titlebar

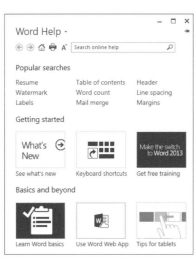

You'll see a variety of useful items all related to Word. Open the Help window from Excel, and you will see similar items, but tailored specifically to Excel.

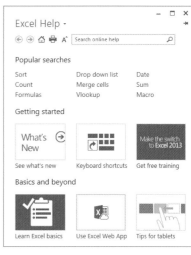

When you are offline, you get Basic Office help only.

Don't forget

To get the full content for Help topics, you must have an internet connection. Otherwise you'll have only Offline help which offers very basic information (see page 212).

Explore Help Topics

1 Enter keywords for a search topic, or select one of the Popular searches, for example, Word count

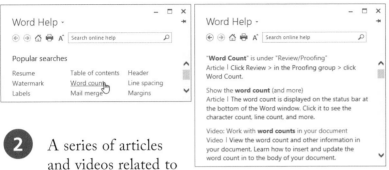

2 A series of articles and videos related to the topic are listed

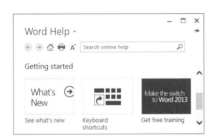

3 The Getting Started section has links to a video and article on new features in Word 2013, an article on Keyboard Shortcuts and a series of training videos

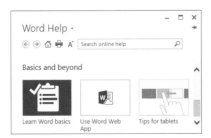

4 The Basics and beyond section introduces basic tasks in Word and in the Word Web App, plus Tips for tablets, a link to the Office Touch Guide

Unlike previous versions of Microsoft Office, the Help offered is not context sensitive, so you always start with the same selection of items.

Whichever topic you select, you will still have the Search box so you can locate new topics, or click the Home button to return to the initial Help window.

Offline Help

1 If you have no Internet connection when you select Office Help, you get the limited Offline Basic Help

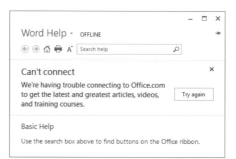

2 To see the Offline Help even when connected, click the down arrow and select Help from your computer

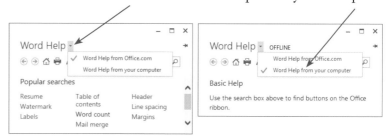

3 Enter a search term, e.g. print, and press Enter to get basic information about Print buttons on the Ribbon

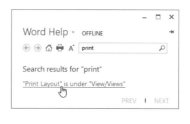

4 Click the result to get any extra details, such as the shortcut keys

Developer Tab

The Developer tab provides access to functions that are useful if you want to create or run macros or develop applications to use with Office programs. It is aimed at the advanced user and for this reason, it is normally hidden.

To reveal the Developer tab in a particular Office application:

1 Open the application and select the File tab, then click Options

2 In the Options for that application, select Customize Ribbon

Don't forget

Enabling the Developer tab for one Office application does not enable it in any of the other applications. You must enable (or disable) the Developer tab for each application individually.

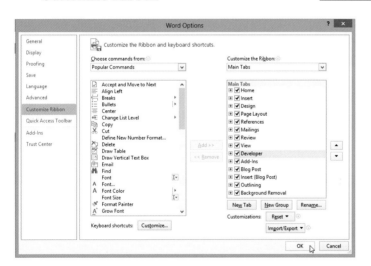

Hot tip

The selection of groups included in the Developer tab varies by application. For example, Word has the 6 shown, Excel has 5 and PowerPoint has 4.

3 Click the Developer box, which is initially unticked, and then click OK, and the Developer tab is added

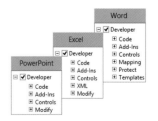

Remove Personal Details

There can be more in the file version of an Office document than the information that appears when you review or print it. If the document has been subject to revision, there could be a record of all changes, including original or deleted text and data and any comments added by reviewers.

1 Select Review, and click the No Markup button

Hot tip

The markup includes all the changes and comments that have been applied, and may give away more information than you'd really like.

2 Select All Markup and you'll see that the file has the original text as well as the changes and comments

If you share online copies of the document, you may not want such information included. Office 2013 makes it easy to completely remove such information from the published versions of the document.

3 Select File, Save as, enter a new name for the document and click the Save button

Beware

Do not make changes to your master document. It is best to work with a copy of the document, to avoid the possibility of accidently removing too much information.

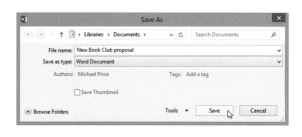

4 Select the File tab, click Info, then click the Check for Issues button, and select Inspect Document

Don't forget

You can also check for accessibility issues and compatibility issues, before making your document available.

5 Click Remove All for each item in turn, where unwanted or unnecessary data was found

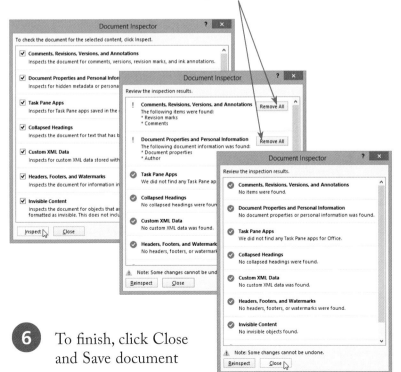

Hot tip

Select those elements that may contain hidden information that you want to remove. You might allow items, such as headers, footers and watermarks, if detected.

Don't forget

If you've used a working copy, the information will still be available in the original document, just in case it's needed.

6 To finish, click Close and Save document

Protect Your Documents

At the simplest level, you could tell users that the document has been completed, and should no longer be changed.

1 Open the document, select the File tab, click Info, and Protect Document, and select Mark as Final

Don't forget

When you send out a document, you might want to discourage or prevent others from making unauthorized changes to content.

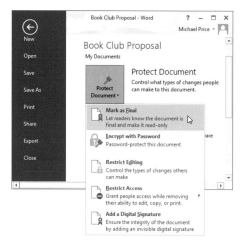

Don't forget

Another way to make the document read-only is to publish it using the PDF, or XPS document format (see page 199).

2 Click OK to confirm and complete the action

3 The effects of marking as final are explained

Hot tip

The Ribbon and all its commands are hidden, and the Info for the document confirms the new status.

4 When you next open the document, you see Read-Only on the title bar, along with a warning message

...cont'd

Alternatively, you might choose to encrypt the document, to prohibit unauthorized changes.

1 From Info, Protect Document, select Encrypt with Password

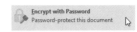

2 Provide a password for the document, click OK, re-enter the password to confirm, and click OK again

217

3 Contents haven't been altered, but when you close the document, you are still prompted to save changes

4 Now, anyone who wants to open the document will be prompted to enter the password and click OK to continue

If you want to remove the encryption at any time:

1 Open the document (with password) and reselect Encrypt with Password

2 Delete the password then click OK and Save

Beware

If you lose the password, the document cannot be recovered, so you should work with a copy, and retain the original document in secure storage.

Don't forget

With encryption applied, no one will be able to review or change the document without the correct password, as will be indicated in the document Info.

Protect Document
A password is required to open this document.

Restrict Permission

You can go further and apply specific levels of protection.

1 Working with a copy of your document, click File, Info, Protect Document, and select Restrict Editing

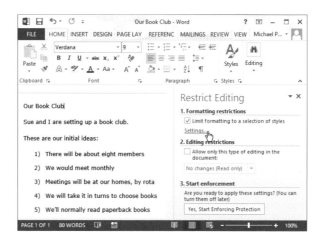

You can also click the Review tab and the Restrict Editing button to display this pane.

2 The Restrict Editing task pane appears

When you have selected the styles that are allowed, you can choose to remove any existing formatting or styles that would now be disallowed.

3 Choose to Limit formatting to a selection of styles, and click Settings, to say what styles you want in the document

4 Choose to Allow this type of editing in the document, and select the level

You can give specific users permission to freely edit particular sections of the document.

5 Click the button Yes, Start Enforcing Protection

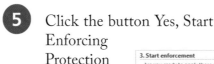

6 Choose the protection method. For home use, select Password (supplying a revised password if desired)

7 Other users are required to enter the password to edit the document at the level permitted

The user is warned if the document is already locked for editing by another user, and can make a local copy or wait for notification.

For businesses with domains and servers, User authentication allows specific editing functions to be associated with particular users, using Information Rights Management (IRM) facilities.

This is not available to home or business systems that do not use domains and servers.

If you have existing IRM protected documents from a previous version of Office, you can continue to use the service, even without server capabilities.

Finally, an invisible digital signature can ensure integrity.

8 Click File, Info, Protect Document, Add a Digital Signature

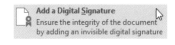

Don't forget

File, Info will now show that certain types of changes are restricted in this document.

Hot tip

You can also click File, Info, Protect document, and select Restrict Access to use IRM to give specific capabilities to selected users.

Don't forget

You'll need to obtain a digital ID from one of the suppliers at the Office Marketplace. Some offer trial versions so you can experiment with the service.

Trust Center

The Trust Center contains security and privacy settings for Office applications. To open the Trust Center:

1 Select File, Options, and then select Trust Center

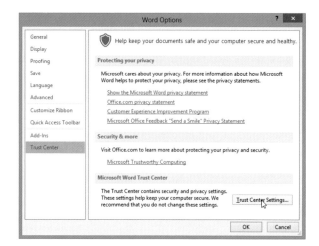

2 Click the Trust Center Settings button and choose an option, for example Macro Settings, to see details

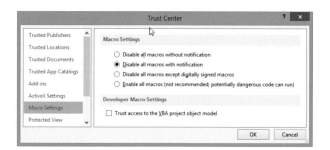

3 Select Add-ins to apply more stringent controls

12 Where Next?

This provides a quick overview of other Office applications that may be in your edition, and products that integrate with Office, or that share its formats. Finally, we look at the online Office Web Apps .

Other Office Applications

We have looked at the main Office applications (Word, Excel, PowerPoint, Outlook, and OneNote) and the Office Tools in some detail, and taken a quick preview of Access and Publisher. Depending on which edition of Office you install, you may have other applications included.

Office 2013 RT
RT Home & Student
Office 2013
H&S Home & Student
H&B Home & Business
Std Standard
Pro Professional
Pro+ Professional Plus
Office 365
Home Home Premium
   University
Bus Small Business
   Professional Plus
   Enterprise
Office 2013 Web
Web Office Web Apps

Outlook 2013 has been added to the applications included with Windows RT 8.1.

All the applications are also available in stand-alone editions. This is the only way to get the Project and Visio applications.

Office 2013 RT	RT8	RT8.1			
Office 2013	H&S	H&B	Std	Pro	Pro+
Office 365				Home	Bus
Office 2013 Web	Web				
Word	Y	Y	Y	Y	Y
Excel	Y	Y	Y	Y	Y
PowerPoint	Y	Y	Y	Y	Y
OneNote	Y	Y	Y	Y	Y
Outlook	–	Y	Y	Y	Y
Publisher	–	–	Y	Y	Y
Access	–	–	–	Y	Y
InfoPath	–	–	–	–	Y
Lync	–	–	–	–	Y
Project	–	–	–	–	–
Visio	–	–	–	–	–

Office 2013 Professional Plus or any Office 365 business edition will offer the most complete set of applications:

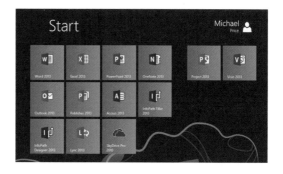

This also shows the two stand-alone only applications.

Office 2013 and Office 365

The major difference between these two Office suites is the pricing and licensing mechanisms. Office 2013 editions are purchased for a one-time fee, and no more payment is required until you update to a new version. The purchase entitles you to use the software on one computer only. Office 365 uses a subscription method, so you pay a yearly charge based on the edition you choose. This entitles you to use the software on up to five computers, and you can apply upgrades whenever they become available.

Both suites contain selections from the same set of applications, though as the table shows, Office 365 editions include more products than Office 2013 Home editions.

Larger businesses will normally choose Office 365, but the Office suite most suitable for home or smaller business use depends on how many licenses you need, how often you expect to upgrade the applications and which specific applications and services you require.

To compare the suites:

1 Go to **office.microsoft.com** and select Products

2 Select the Compare link for Home or for Business

If your system is always connected via Wi-Fi or via the mobile network, you can also consider a fully online solution using the Office Web Apps (see page 230) if these offer enough function to meet your needs.

223

The Office editions for the larger businesses and enterprises are available on a per user basis and offer advanced corporate services.

...cont'd

Don't forget

Prices vary according to your region. In the examples the prices are for the United States and correct at the time of printing.

3 Locate and select the link to Compare Office suites

4 Review the charges and features for the editions of Office 2013 and Office 2013 displayed

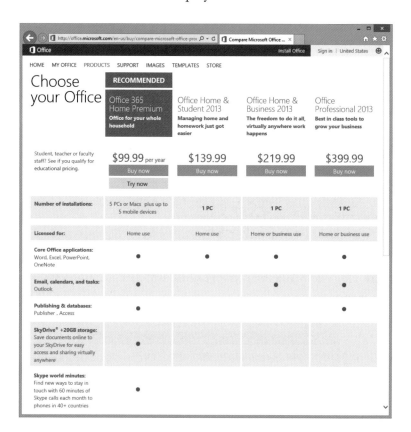

5 Decide on your requirements and identify your options and their relative costs

As the example scenarios indicate, if you need more than a couple of licenses, or require the fuller set of products, or want to upgrade more often than every five years, you are very likely to find Office 365 Home Premium the best choice for home use.

Hot tip

Example scenarios:

2 PCs, 5 years between upgrades, basic set of products:

Office 365 HP $500

Office 2013 H&S $280

2 PCs, 5 years between upgrades, fuller set of products:

Office 365 HP $500

Office 2013 Pro $800

SkyDrive and SkyDrive Pro

Office 2013 can use your SkyDrive (see page 18). This is online storage associated with your Microsoft account and managed on your behalf by Microsoft at **www.skydrive.com** SkyDrive is available to any user who registers a Microsoft account, and the service offers up to 7GB of free storage. Additional storage is available for an annual charge. With SkyDrive you can work with your data files from any computer with Office 2013 or via the Web browser using the Office Web Apps (see page 230).

Don't forget

The price varies according to your region. In the United States, the annual charge is $10 for 20 GB of additional storage. (*Prices correct at the time of printing.*)

There are apps available to allow you to access your SkyDrive files using your mobile phone. There are also Windows apps available to manage local copies of your SkyDrive files and folders, so that you can continue to work even when offline, knowing that the documents will be automatically synced the next time you connect.

For business users, Microsoft provides the SkyDrive Pro app. This supports storage that is hosted and managed by your business organization, using SharePoint Server software. The

storage may also be hosted on the Internet, using SharePoint Online services.

You store and organize work documents or other files in your personal SkyDrive Pro library, and from there you can share files and collaborate on documents with co-workers.

Hot tip

With SharePoint Online, each user has 7GB of personal storage capacity allocated to them. For on-premises SharePoint 2013 setups, the per-user storage capacity is a configurable parameter that the site administrators will manage.

Stand-alone Applications

There are some applications that are part of Microsoft Office 2013, but are not included in any of the Office editions.

Project

This is a specialized product that provides all the software tools and functions you require to manage and control a project. It handles schedules and finances, helps keep project teams on target, and integrates with other Office applications and may be supported by Office Project Server.

Don't forget

The file extension for Project 2013 is .mpp, and it is also compatible with Project 2010. Project 2007 and Project 2000–2003 use the same extension, but are treated as separate file types.

Visio

This is drawing and diagramming software, to help you visualize and communicate complex information. It provides a wide range of templates, including business process flowcharts, network diagrams, workflow diagrams, database models, and software diagrams, and makes use of predefined SmartShapes symbols. There are sample diagrams, with data integrated to provide context, helping you decide which template suits your requirements.

Don't forget

Visio 2013 is available in two editions. Standard offers the basic set of diagramming tools. Professional adds real-time dynamic visuals. The Visio Premium found in previous versions is no longer offered.

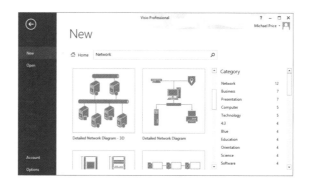

MapPoint 2013

MapPoint applications can be integrated into Office 2013 applications. There are two main MapPoint products:

MapPoint North America 2013

Microsoft MapPoint software includes detailed geographic coverage for the United States, Canada, and Mexico (but the Address Find feature was not available for Mexico at the time of printing). Mapping coverage outside of those regions is limited to political boundaries and populated places.

You may have some pre-req items to install before you can install MapPoint itself.

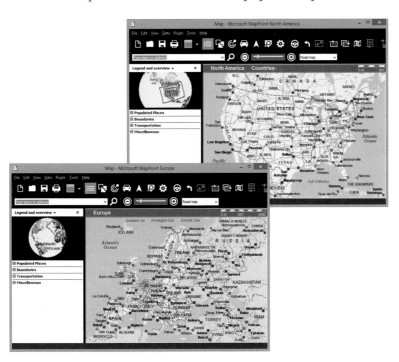

MapPoint 2013 Europe

This provides detailed street-level mapping and address-find capability for Austria, Belgium, Denmark, Finland, France, Germany, Greece, Italy, Luxembourg, the Netherlands, Norway, Portugal, Spain, Sweden, Switzerland, and the United Kingdom.

In addition, MapPoint Europe provides some street-level coverage, but does not support address-find, for various countries ranging from Andorra to Vatican City.

There are 14-day free trialsavailable as downloads. See **www.microsoft.com/ mappoint** for details.

Using MapPoint with Office

When you install MapPoint, add-ins are installed into Office applications, so you can use MapPoint 2013 to insert maps into Office documents and presentations directly from the application. To insert a map into a Word 2013 document:

Don't forget

MapPoint is designed to work with Microsoft Office programs to create maps from data stored in an Office document or database and to insert maps into documents and presentations.

1 Open the document, select Insert, then click the Object button in the Text group

2 From Object, select MapPoint 2013 Map, OK

3 The selected version of MapPoint will open

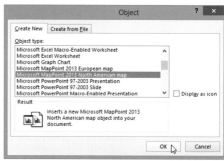

4 Locate the map section required for the document, using the MapPoint 2013 menus and toolbar

5 Select File, Exit & Return to Document

Hot tip

Double-click the map to open MapPoint and make any required changes to the map.

6 The map is inserted and the document can be finished and saved

Working with Other Products

Applications that do not directly integrate with Microsoft Office may accept files in Office document formats, as input. E.g. to place a Word document in Adobe InDesign CS6:

1 Start InDesign and open a document (new or existing)

2 Select File, Place

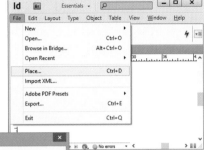

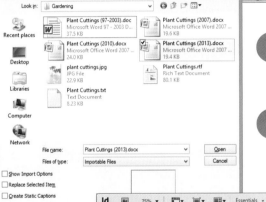

3 Navigate to a required Word file

4 Select the file and click Open

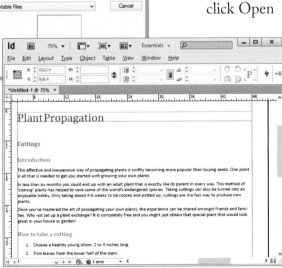

5 To override Word styles, create InDesign styles with the same names as the Word styles, and these will be used when the Word document is placed

229

The InDesign document will not necessarily have many paragraph styles defined, initially.

The InDesign document will inherit the paragraph styles used in the Word document.

Office Web Apps

If you have a Microsoft Account and associated SkyDrive, you can use Office Web Apps to create or access your Office documents from a browser, and share files and collaborate with other users online. You don't even need a copy of Office on the machine that you are using.

If you aren't currently signed in to a Microsoft account, you'll be asked to sign in (or sign up for an account).

To use Office Web Apps:

1 Open Internet Explorer and go to **www.skydrive.com** If you are signed in to your Microsoft account (as when using Windows 8) your SkyDrive appears

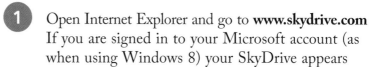

Don't forget

In SkyDrive, select Create and choose an Office Web App to create a Word, Excel, PowerPoint, or OneNote document in the current folder using the browser.

2 Open a folder and select an existing Word document

3 The document opens in Reading view in the browser

4 Select Edit Document and Edit in Word Web App

5 The document is opened for editing in the browser

6 The Word Web App has limited function, so to get the full capabilities select Open in Word

7 Select an Excel spreadsheet from SkyDrive to open in the browser

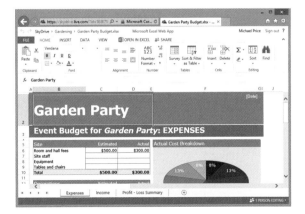

Select Edit Document, Edit in Word to open the document in Microsoft Word.

If you do not have Word 2013 installed, you'll get an error message.

You'll be warned if there are features that are not handled by the Office Web App version of the application.

My Office

Hot tip

My Office provides you with another way to access your documents and the Office Web Apps from your browser.

1 Go to the website **office.microsoft.com** and select My Office

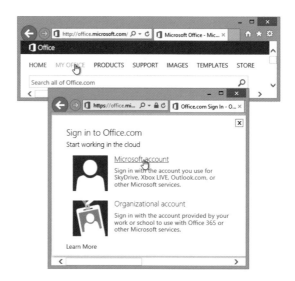

2 You are prompted to sign in using your Microsoft Account (or the Corporate account for Office 365)

Don't forget

Recent documents are displayed, along with a link to your SkyDrive.

Don't forget

Scroll down and you'll see shortcuts to create documents using any of the four Office Web Apps, along with links to Recent folders.

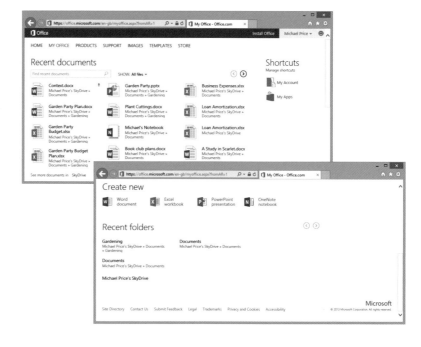

P

Q

R

S

U

V

W

X, Y, Z